# TRY NOT TO THINK OF A PINK ELEPHANT

## Stories about OCD

First published 2022 by
FREMANTLE PRESS.

Fremantle Press Inc. trading as Fremantle Press
PO Box 158, North Fremantle, Western Australia, 6159
fremantlepress.com.au

Cover images by Julia Garan, istockphoto.com
Cover design by Nada Backovic, nadabackovic.com
Printed and bound by IPG

A catalogue record for this
book is available from the
NATIONAL LIBRARY
OF AUSTRALIA National Library of Australia

ISBN 9781760991982 (paperback)
ISBN 9781760991999 (ebook)

Department of
**Local Government, Sport
and Cultural Industries**
GOVERNMENT OF
WESTERN AUSTRALIA

Fremantle Press is supported by the State Government through the
Department of Local Government, Sport and Cultural Industries.

Fremantle Press respectfully acknowledges the Whadjuk people of
the Noongar nation as the Traditional Owners and Custodians of the
land where we work in Walyalup.

# TRY NOT TO THINK OF A PINK ELEPHANT

## Stories about OCD

Martin Ingle
Dani Leever
Patrick Marlborough
Katharine Pollock
Sienna Rose Scully
Introduction by Kimberley Quinlan

 FREMANTLE PRESS

# Content warning

These personal stories discuss anxiety, depression, obsessive compulsive disorder (OCD) and, in particular, the behaviours associated with OCD. They are intended for readers from a range of ages and lived experiences. Please take care when reading.

# Contents

# Introduction

Kimberley Quinlan

When I first meet with someone with OCD and begin to educate them on OCD and what OCD treatment entails, it is not uncommon for them to experience myriad strong emotions. Some feel a tremendous sense of relief and hope as they finally have a name for what they have been experiencing. Others say they feel overwhelmed with sadness and grief because of all the time and important life events lost to OCD.

Statistics show that approximately three per cent of Australians have OCD.[1] However, most people with OCD report that they feel like they are the only ones, not knowing anyone who has experienced such terrifying intrusive and repetitive thoughts, feelings, sensations and urges.

Many people with OCD, including some of the authors in this book, struggle to get a correct diagnosis simply because they do not wash their hands or jump over cracks. Unfortunately, there are still many misconceptions about the symptoms and diagnostic criteria of OCD. As a result, anger and regret may be the predominant emotion because the person with OCD has struggled alone for so long and wished that someone could have saved them from all the suffering they have endured. If you experience any or all of these emotions, please know these emotions are a normal part of OCD recovery.

In this anthology, you will learn that there are many different presentations of OCD. These include obsessions about harm, sexuality, religion, morals, health, relationships, and existential concerns, just to name a few. In fact, obsessions can target any area of your life, commonly showing up in the areas that you value the most.

---

1 Australian Bureau of Statistics (2008. *National Survey of Mental Health and Wellbeing: Summary of Results, 2007* (2008), p.27.

OCD recovery involves learning how to outsmart one's OCD. You might even consider OCD treatment and OCD recovery a game that you can win by understanding the tricks OCD uses to keep you in the obsessive and compulsive cycle. A crucial part of this process is acknowledging that OCD recovery is *not* about getting rid of your intrusive thoughts, feelings, sensations, images and urges. Just like the title of this book, science shows that the more you try not to think about something (like a pink elephant), the more you end up thinking about it. Go ahead and see for yourself! The act of trying not to think about something involves you thinking about it, keeping you stuck in a loop of torment and confusion.

Instead of running from obsessions, you will also learn how to break the OCD cycle by facing your fear, uncertainty and doubt, one obsession at a time. Outsmarting OCD involves learning to tolerate discomfort with compassion instead of beating yourself up or punishing yourself.

It also involves learning to resist the urge to engage in compulsive safety behaviours such as physical behaviours, avoidance, reassurance-seeking and mental rumination to eliminate or reduce the discomfort you feel.

This therapy modality is called Exposure and Response Prevention and is considered the gold-standard treatment for OCD. Every day, I have the honour of watching people with OCD learn how to take back their life from OCD. They practise standing up to their OCD, and they use their many wonderful personality and character traits to build a life where OCD doesn't make their choices or determine how boldly they live.

It is my honour to introduce you to a selection of writings that demonstrate what OCD recovery looks like for different people. In this anthology, you will get to walk alongside these wonderfully courageous and talented humans as they share how they have navigated life with their own variety of obsessions and compulsions. Sienna, Katharine, Martin, Patrick and Dani all share their wins and losses to OCD. They share their journey of navigating relationships, hobbies, careers and identities while managing the torment of obsessions and compulsions.

First, you will hear Sienna Rose Scully's story about how OCD interfered with her most valued relationships. Sienna beautifully provides a roadmap for those who are new to OCD. She shares important information about OCD treatment, including the key concepts that helped her throughout her OCD recovery.

Second, you will hear Katharine Pollock's story. Katharine creatively shares how certain TV characters and musicians helped her conceptualise her OCD, health anxiety, perfectionism and an eating disorder. Katharine also shares the valuable practices and lessons that have helped her along the way.

Next, Martin Ingles tells his OCD story using a timeline of love stories. From my experience of treating OCD, OCD's biggest casualty is people's most valued relationships. Martin does an amazing job sharing how OCD shaped many of his relationships and inspires us all to never give up on love.

Patrick Marlborough, who has the fourth story of this anthology, takes us into their experience of OCD and a number of other neurodivergent diagnoses. Patrick insightfully and humorously compares and contrasts the different ways Australia and the United States of America conceptualise mental health and shares their lived experience of managing OCD and other conditions in those environments.

Lastly, Dani Leever shares how OCD can shift from moment to moment. Their thoughtful, journal-like account will validate how difficult it is to resist the urge to engage in compulsions. Anyone with OCD will feel very inspired and validated by Dani's story.

These very personal stories provide a unique window into how OCD can target different areas of one's life while also showing us that there are very individual pathways in which sufferers, with support and understanding, can design their own OCD recovery.

If you have OCD, or are close to someone who does, my wish is that each of these stories brings you a deep sense of hope, knowing it is possible to live a full, rich life even while having OCD.

# OCD: Anxiety's Misunderstood Best Friend

Sienna Rose Scully

*For Olivia, Priya, my younger self, and all of you out there who will hopefully find some comfort in these words.*

**CONTENT WARNING FOR YOUNGER READERS**

This piece discusses anxiety, depression, and obsessive compulsive disorder (OCD) and, in particular, the behaviours associated with OCD.

## Author's note

I have written my story for readers—particularly teenagers or even younger readers—who may have OCD and are contemplating the details of this for the first time. Please be aware that the details of what it is like to experience OCD, anxiety and depression may be triggering for you.

I have written this also for the parents and caregivers of those with OCD, so that you might have insight into what a young person is going through, though that young person may not yet be in a position to articulate these complex emotions and concepts.

I tell you my story because I wish there had been something like this for me to read when I was younger, to help me understand that I was not crazy and I was not alone. As I have grown into adulthood, I have come to understand what OCD is and how it tries to rule your life. I have also come to learn that it is possible for this not to be so. To know there is hope and light, and you can still achieve all the things you wish to achieve. I hope my story can do for you what I wish it could have done for me at a younger age.

## A Little Green-Eyed Girl

A young girl looks up through the window of the backseat of a car. Flashes of leaves and branches covering the darkening afternoon sky. Silhouettes of trees all but a blur as she stares into the endless sky, thinking about death. A girl as young as six at the very beginning of her life, thinking about life's end. Having an existential crisis while having not existed for more than a long-running television series. Knowing and understanding that life ends and feeling complete curiosity and dread at not knowing what happens when it does. However … hers is not a fear for what will happen to her. It is a fear for what will happen to her mother. She needs to understand life's biggest mystery because this six-year-old does not want her beloved mum to die.

This young girl is me. All of my earliest memories have this one common theme: anxiety at the fear of losing my mum. I do not know why I had this immense anxiety about wanting to make sure that my mum was safe and not wanting to lose her, because she was not the type of parent that made a child worry. She was not the type of parent who made the child do the parenting, so why, for as long as I could remember, did I have this anxiety and need to make sure she was safe?

My mum was an amazing mother. Full of wisdom, creativity, fun and depth. She held me and my three siblings to essential standards of kindness and compassion, and instilled within us the importance of education. I will never be able to encompass all of what my mum was with mere words on a page. Only those who were lucky enough to have known her will understand her unique brilliance, and the spirit of life she embodied. But although my mum provided us a warm, loving environment to grow in, I still had an irrational and immense anxiety around her dying, and not wanting her to die.

Although I can remember this anxiety from the very beginning of my memories, when I was about eight or nine, my anxiety began to insist on me performing a series of physical actions so that I could prevent my mum from dying. The voice inside me said: *If I do this, then my mum will be safe and won't die* and it also said: *If I don't do it, then she will die.* And so, anxiety's best friend, OCD, decided to join the friendship group and oh, was it clingy …

Anxiety already had kept me company for a long while. It is not unusual for children to experience anxiety from time to time— the kind that might be described as a feeling of unease, worry or nervousness about things with an uncertain outcome such as a first day of school or going to the dentist. But some kids, like me, can experience an ongoing and constant (or chronic) anxiety. That is the kind of anxiety that kept me company: these are feelings that are a lot more excessive, persistent, and so intense they can result in anxiety attacks (also known as panic attacks). The physical symptoms that can come with this anxiety are rapid breathing (hyperventilation), sweating, trembling, excessive weakness and tiredness, trouble concentrating and sleeping and even stomach (gastrointestinal) problems. This makes anxiety even more difficult to have around because it not only likes to cause mental problems but physical problems too.

A disorder is something that disrupts normal physical or mental functions. Obsessive compulsive disorder (OCD) is characterised by unwanted recurring thoughts (or obsessions) that result in rituals or actions (compulsive responses) that are aimed at dissolving the unwanted thoughts. So, the voice inside me said: *When you close that door, you have to open and close it three times or your mum will die.* Although over the years my unwanted thoughts varied, my most frequently recurring unwanted thoughts heavily revolved around thoughts like these about the safety of my mum and her dying.

When I was eight, I was unaware of what OCD was and completely confused by its arrival. All of a sudden OCD was here without an invitation, and it had the audacity to be extremely bossy. It was as if a very unwanted house guest had taken up residence in my mind. OCD was a stranger that wouldn't introduce itself properly to me and never explained who it was, where it had come from or how long it planned to stay. Not knowing what it was, I was convinced I was crazy because I didn't know of anyone else who had such an unwanted guest in their mind too, and I was too afraid to ask.

When I finally began to learn some things about anxiety's best friend, I discovered that OCD is not only clingy, but misunderstood as well. People believe they know what OCD is, but often, they are wrong. And so when I finally got to a point in my life that I thought I knew what OCD was, I still thought I was crazy. This was because I bought the popular misconception that OCD referred to people who just loved things to be neat and tidy. So, I still wasn't aware that what I had was *actual* OCD. I wish I had been able to learn years earlier than I did that I was not crazy and that my unwanted guest had a name, and that there was help for people like me.

## Numbers

Picture eight-year-old Sienna, sitting on the toilet, feet swinging, barely able to touch the floor. This is when anxiety first invited its best friend to the party and I was unwillingly introduced. I know I was around eight years old because of the house we were living in at the time. Thinking back, I used to perhaps blame the multiplication chart on the back of the toilet door for which number was going to dictate my compulsions for that following period of time. (I had never been great at math anyway so why not blame the kookaburra trying to teach me my times tables?) But it wasn't the kookaburra's fault, it was the beginning of an anxiety disorder that was going to test me for years to come.

The toilet might seem like a funny place for things to start. An individually enclosed toilet, with that hot-pink multiplication chart bordered by various Australian animals staring at me. It's a vivid memory (though I wish I could actually remember the multiplications and not just the wombat hugging the emu). It was in that enclosed space that I can remember certain numbers began to hold a certain importance. Though I didn't know it then, it was OCD that would dictate the amount of toilet paper squares I could use (or had to use even if unneeded; even then, I cared about the environment, I swear, but unfortunately OCD didn't get the memo on the whole reduce, reuse, recycle …). The particular number changed all the time, however I remember periods of 3 and 9 being important and, as I grew older, the number 4 became very insistent. This number became the safety net in the beginning of my journey with OCD. Once I completed the compulsions and rituals the right amount of times, using the current dictated number, then I was finally free for at least a little while until the next unwanted thought broke its way into my head. Sometimes there would be a change in the numbers but I would only find out after I had completed the compulsions and still didn't feel free and relaxed. OCD was letting me know that I had to either keep going with the compulsions or start the compulsions again to find the new number that would become my safety net.

If you are reading this as someone *without* OCD, perhaps a parent or a friend of someone with OCD, I am going to try my best to help you understand what people with this disorder endure. One of the most important things you can do is to make sure that you continue reading this with an open mind and a willingness to support the person you know with OCD, because I hope my story will give you some insight into just how tiring and trying it is.

As I briefly touched on earlier, I am the youngest of four children born within five years of each other. I am the only one of my siblings who suffers from OCD. This is not to say that they may not suffer from their own troubles, just that I was the lucky winner of the OCD raffle. I always knew I was different from my siblings but did not understand why.

If you are reading this as someone just discovering their OCD, it is okay to know that although your siblings may not suffer from the same disorder, you are not alone. And, if you are a parent or caregiver, understand that just because one of your kids doesn't have OCD, it doesn't mean that none of them will. OCD does not discriminate and does not care about your gender or the colour of your hair, or whether you are the youngest, oldest or middle child ... OCD is something you're born with: it is caused by the particular chemical, structural and functional aspects of the brain. It's not something that you can catch—if you do have OCD, it was most likely always going to pop up at some stage in your childhood, and it seems to appear in people who are more anxiety prone.

## Rituals

OCD is the very outspoken guest who insists things are done their way. It appears out of nowhere with its suitcase of rituals (compulsions) that must be done in a very specific way. Sometimes the suitcase is light with only a few rituals in there, and at other times that suitcase is stuffed to the brim, containing an overwhelming amount that OCD is determined *must* be completed.

When I describe some of the many rituals that OCD has pulled from that suitcase, if you have OCD, you may laugh in recognition. Or perhaps you will just find some comfort in understanding that these compulsions you have been dealing with all by yourself do not make you crazy, they make you a unique and strong individual who is going through the race of life with an extra twenty kilograms strapped to your back (and which can sometimes feel like an extra fifty or one hundred or even 999,999,999 kilograms). My own rituals have changed and evolved over time. Sometimes it has been a slight change in an existing ritual and sometimes it's a completely new ritual that OCD pulls from the bag. The thing they have in common though is that they must be completed. I'll give OCD that much—it's a consistent little sh*t.

My relationship with OCD has evolved as I have grown. OCD has aged with me, having different triggers as I have entered and experienced different parts of my life. There have been countless rituals since I began my journey with OCD, but I am not going to go over each one, just share some of my favourites (and by 'favourites' I mean the rituals that mentally demolished me and almost always wore me out over time).

## The Walls

The walls was one of my earliest rituals. We had moved to a new house (we moved a lot, and no, that is not why I have OCD). This was after the house where I first felt compelled to enact rituals and compulsions based on the multiplication chart in the toilet. I would have been around ten or eleven years old. The most defining moment of my life at this time was the death of my puppa (my mum's dad), who was like a father to me and my siblings, and with whom my mum was extremely close. It hit us all very hard and was my first experience of grief.

At this house, the suitcase of OCD rituals became very full. OCD insisted that when I was walking past a wall I *had* to touch it. And I had to touch it a certain number of times before I could move on. This was the beginning of thinking I must be crazy as I just had to touch these walls. OCD said if I did not, then I was not allowed to go on with my day, which at that age might have only involved climbing a tree or building a fort, but not being able to naturally flow with your day has a really big impact, no matter the age. It could happen at home or at school, where I had to try even harder to hide it. It was at this point that I also found out what would happen if I tried to resist it—because I tried, and oh I tried.

### Running to a Particular Point and Touching

To explain this particular ritual, I would like to tell you about how the obsession (or unwanted thought) relates to the compulsion (the ritual or action). The intense need to complete these rituals comes from intrusive, recurring, unwanted thoughts that squirm their way into the mind of the OCD sufferer out of nowhere. The unwanted thought could come at any time and have no relation to what you are doing whatsoever: for example you are a reading a book and now all of a sudden if you don't reread the whole page (aka complete the compulsion) a certain number of times then your grandma will have a stroke, or your friend will get in a car accident, or your brother will stop breathing in his sleep. These unwanted thoughts vary in severity and in the amount of distress they cause.

If you suffer from OCD and are reading this, I need you to know that these thoughts *are. not. you!* These thoughts are a symptom of the OCD and they are not who you are. They do not define you as a person and they have nothing to do with the kind, exceptional human being that you are. I am telling you this because I wish someone had told *me* this when I was younger. Even if this is the only thing you take away from this piece, then that is good. It is something I need you to know and be aware of! You are you, and the OCD is the unwanted guest that has locked itself away inside a room of your mind, swallowed the key and refuses to leave. And not only is it refusing to leave but it randomly decides to start playing its loud, obnoxious, whiny, deep bass music at any time of the day or night and won't shut the f**k up! Unlike you, it never seems to get tired.

Around this time, the certain ritual of running to a particular point came into play. My unwanted thoughts have varied over the years but, as I have said, the biggest most common one was that if I did not complete the ritual then my mum would die. With this compulsion, I could be doing anything at all and then the random unwanted thought, paired with the compulsion that I *had* to follow, would shoot into my mind. Many times it would have to do with running to a particular point and touching it (sometimes a certain amount of times, *hellooo*, numbers) and making it back in a certain amount of time.

One of the most vivid examples I remember is from when I was around ten or eleven listening to music in my room. All of a sudden OCD let me know that I would have to run outside to the tree outside my window and back before the song ended or my mum would die. OCD doesn't play fair and works against you in trying to finish the compulsion. It doesn't want you to succeed. It will wait until there is only fifteen seconds left in the song or it will make you run to that particular tree but this time touching it three times isn't enough, you now have to touch it six times and with a particular pattern and you know if you mess it up then you definitely have to start all over again. Or maybe it doesn't want you to run to that tree, it wants you to run to that area and then only be able to leave when your feet have felt you adjusting your weight on each foot a particular number of times and you have the sensation that you can finally leave. I remember the terrible feeling of not making it back in time before the song ended … I felt as if I had killed my own mother. Her death may not occur right away, but it was as if I had caused the curse to be placed upon her so that she maybe wouldn't drop down right at that moment, but if she ever got into a car accident or slipped and hit her head or got cancer, then I knew it would be my fault.

Paired with that feeling of guilt at failure came the 'make-up' compulsions. OCD has a back-up suitcase full of other rituals you can try to do when you failed to properly do the rituals from the first suitcase. You feel the need to scour through this back-up suitcase and do these compulsions to try to reverse the others that you have unsuccessfully done. Rarely do these make-up compulsions make you feel better. Instead, you just keep having to do them until you're too mentally exhausted to fully feel the sensation of being condemned at its most painful and weighty.

## The Light Switch

The light switch is one of my all-time 'favourites'. This compulsion started around the same time as those described above, however, unlike them, it stuck with me for years. The thing about light switches is that they are in *every. single. room.* The days (*ahem* years *ahem*) of not being able to turn a light switch on and off without doing it a certain number of times were some of the most excruciating of my life. In the depths of my most severe bouts of OCD (which I will get into later) I was unable to remove myself from the light switch as I never received the sensation of the compulsion being complete and would call to my godmother to please help and physically remove me. The fact that I can now normally operate a light switch brings me so much relief, though it might seem a tiny thing to people who have not suffered from OCD. The feeling of being able to normally operate something that your OCD had once had control over is a massive accomplishment. This also shows how over time your rituals can evolve and change. Something like a light switch that for years had a hold on you, can once again become nothing but the utility that turns on and off the lights. It shows how random and debilitating a compulsion can be. OCD can take a common activity and suddenly make it something that is exhaustingly time-consuming, along with creating a fear about when you will next have to use the object or utility.

The amount of time needed to complete these rituals takes a massive toll on a person—whether it is trying to go to bed without performing an hour of rituals (yes, sometimes I have tried to go to bed and am still unable to hours later due to OCD, no matter how early I have to get up the next morning) or missing your bus because you're stuck trying to turn the light on and off and on and off and on and off and on and off…

As I was reaching adolescence, it felt as if anxiety and OCD teamed up and forced me to wear the third part of a 'Best Friends Forever' necklace. It was an extremely heavy necklace and one I wished I could take off, even though in lots of other ways I was feeling happy and grateful with my life. Of course, as many families face, there were also certain other heavy family issues present in my life. But despite all this, I was still consciously grateful for the mother and home and family I had. I had a childhood of Australian beach fun, I was attending a primary school that I absolutely adored from years four to seven, and I was going on almost yearly family holidays to Melbourne to visit with my loving extended family. At this time before my family broke apart, I felt loved, and I felt as if I belonged. The necklace I wore, I wore in secret and I did not tell anyone of the guest that had come to stay.

At the beginning of high school my family hit a rough patch and my first diagnosis of depression was soon to be made. Anxiety and depression can often come in a package. The effects vary for individuals but depression can feel like a deep cloud of heaviness while anxiety has an effect of heightened emotions and an inability to remain calm. When it comes to unwanted visitors, depression likes to keep company with anxiety too. When having anxiety, you may also experience depression, or you may not. It depends on the individual. For me, even through the height of my depression, my OCD carried on relentlessly. For others, depression has a muting effect that quietens even belligerent OCD for a while.

### Knocking on Wood

Most people know the saying 'knock on wood' or 'touch wood' as a way of making sure you didn't just jinx yourself or someone else, or as a way of taking back what you just said so you don't put it out into the universe. For example, when talking with someone, if you happened to say *I hope my plane doesn't crash tomorrow* you would automatically think *knock on wood* or *touch wood* and find some to touch. Mostly if wood is not around, people will knock on their heads or touch their heads as a superstition.

Before knowing what OCD is, it is easy to think that you are just possibly a very superstitious person and that is definitely how it can come across to others too. When suffering from OCD, it can be nice to think *Oh, I'm just superstitious*, but deep down you might have that niggling feeling that you know it's something more than just superstitions and when you want to hide these rituals, being 'superstitious' becomes the perfect hidden-in-plain-sight label. Another example of this hidden-in-plain-sight label is that perhaps you like to blame your compulsions on being a Virgo or a Capricorn or perhaps continue to assure yourself that Mercury just happens to be in constant retrograde whenever these urges come.

Now it's easy for me to see why a superstition like 'knocking on wood' fit so perfectly into my rituals. This ritual would become heavily present when the various unwanted thoughts would burst into my mind. It could be at any time of the day and as a way of batting off these unwanted thoughts the compulsion would be to knock on wood to make them go away and to prevent the disastrous *something* from happening.

Of course, OCD had to bring numbers into the compulsion. My specific ritual would involve a certain number of knocks on the head and a certain amount of knocks on whatever wood I could find. That could mean shelves, tables, pencils or trees, depending where I was. It was imperative that I find some sort of (preferably unpainted) wood and if that was impossible, then it would mean more knocks on the head to compensate. This compulsion was very prevalent when going to bed so bedside tables and bedframes became common for me to knock on. OCD loves bedtime as the perfect time to open up its suitcase and present to you all these unwanted thoughts and compulsions. It is the time when it has your undivided attention and uses it to its utmost advantage and the time when you are least able to distract yourself. Night-time became a difficult and lonely time and I lay there desperate to be able to simply close my eyes and fall asleep. But that never happened. At night, many of my unwanted thoughts revolved around protecting the ones I love.

A difficult part of the wood-knocking ritual for me was that I sometimes felt the need to involve others in my OCD. This goes against every fibre of your being, which wants to hide the disorder. In my experience, if a friend had mentioned something bad that could happen, you could automatically say 'knock on wood' and they would usually agree and knock on wood or their heads while you laugh together. However, they might not do it the correct number of times, or you might have to keep doing it more than everyone else while trying to hide the fact that you were. In the case of the other person not doing it in a way that fits with your compulsions, it can result in trying to hide this overbearing disorder and at the same time asking your unaware friend to randomly knock on their head two more times or making up for their lack of knocks with more of your own.

Adolescence is a time filled with judgement. Being painfully self-aware of the peculiarity of this disorder as you attempt to complete and hide the compulsions simultaneously, all the while having to navigate this hypercritical landscape is a tiring battle within itself.

### The Walking

This next part of my OCD was—and is still—the most recurring one. This part literally just involved me walking. As anyone would know, as human beings, every single day we are walking places. Sometimes I would be walking and I would catch my reflection (as I grew older, this turned into the mirror compulsion, which I will get to). As I was walking, if I did not catch the right point of my nose in the reflection whilst also thinking of a certain positive memory then I would have to walk backwards and retrace my steps and do the compulsion correctly. Or perhaps I didn't step correctly in the way my OCD wanted me to, in between certain tiles or the number of steps I fit into a certain piece of pavement— this compulsion varied immensely, but you get the picture.

If the walking did not fit with my OCD's compulsion then I would have to walk back and retrace my steps, many times having to walk backwards in the same exact footsteps to do it. This is where the excuses came in.

Walking unfortunately takes place in public places and so the amount of excuses I have made up to friends and family to hide my OCD is countless. There were many times when my friends asked me 'What are you doing?' with a confused look on their faces. My answers varied:

'My shoelace came undone.' *immediately grabs shoe laces*

'I thought I saw something.' *looks around more confused trying to figure out what it was*

'My shoe was coming off.' *kicks shoe onto the ground to try and force foot further inside*

'I stepped wrong on my ankle.' *grabs ankle with hurt face*

I would say anything rather than let my friends or family know what I was actually dealing with, because I was afraid they would not understand.

## Resistance

If you do not have OCD, it might be hard to wrap your head around why you simply can't say no to whatever ritual OCD is proposing. But if you do try to resist, it brings with it an immense wave of anxiety which deepens and gets worse the longer you try to withhold from completing the ritual, and which stops you from focusing on anything else but the ritual and completing it. The most common question from a non-OCD sufferer tends to be: *Then why don't you just not do the rituals?* This is such a difficult thing to try to explain and successfully articulate to someone without the disorder. It might help to think of it this way: the way in which OCD affects our minds is just like the way a broken bone affects someone's physical ability. If you break your leg, you simply *cannot* walk. You cannot use your leg. And people around you can see your leg cast and your crutches and they understand. For people with OCD, asking someone to just *not* do the rituals is like asking someone with a broken leg to walk. When you have a broken leg, you cannot walk even if you want to. When you have OCD, you cannot resist, even if you want to. When you have a broken leg, it hurts to walk. When you have OCD, it hurts to resist. Slowly your leg starts to heal and you can learn to walk again.

Slowly, when you begin to discover what OCD is and seek potential treatment, the acute pain of resisting OCD won't always be so bad. The reason for the rituals is to stop the unwanted thoughts and often to protect the ones we love. For me, it was ultimately a do-or-die situation and if I did not complete the compulsions, then it meant my mum was going to die. I have tried *countless* times over my life to try and simply just not do the compulsions but unfortunately resistance causes severe amounts of distress and the inability to still be able to go on with your day. So even though the compulsions in themselves are mentally exhausting and time-consuming, it is 'easier' to go through that mental exhaustion and moments of relief than to face the mental distress that comes with not doing them. This is why OCD likes to hang around with anxiety. They are a powerful pair of bullies and they thrive on the fact that it is difficult to call them out.

I am going to attempt to explain the exact physical feeling that comes with the compulsions and where that *need* to complete them comes from. For me, when the urge for the compulsion comes, it is not a voice that is telling me exactly what I need to do. Instead, it is a feeling that allows my brain to know in that exact moment what I need to do to (attempt to) get rid of the feeling (to prevent the terrible thing from coming/being true).

Imagine you're sitting in the living room and you're doing your homework and you are focused on that. But then suddenly, of its own accord, the TV comes on blasting a horrifically loud action movie at full volume right next to you. You can't help but notice the sounds that are coming from the TV. You can hear it and it is in every way trying to pull your attention towards it. You can't ignore it. It is simply too loud. The TV is the OCD. When the urge for the compulsion comes, it is like you have this TV blaring in one part of your brain that is demanding attention and is pulling all your focus away from the things you want and *need* to be doing. The only way to turn this TV off is with a complicated instruction manual that contains long lists of illogical, nonsensical instructions. And to make matters worse, the instruction manual is always changing. It is next to impossible to complete your homework while that TV is blaring and so you have to turn it off to continue with your homework. That is what having the urge for compulsions is like. When the TV is on, you cannot continue with your normal day-to-day living. To turn it off is time-consuming, mentally exhausting and physically draining. But you have no choice, otherwise the volume gets louder and louder until you're drowning in the noise.

## Hiding

While all this noise is going on inside your head, on the outside you are doing your utmost to act as if nothing is happening. This is because OCD brings with it an element of shame. Before I tell you more about the rituals that grew and evolved with me into adolescence, I would like to share with you the immense pressure I felt to hide my OCD. For me, hiding began with the awareness that OCD-related behaviours were not 'normal' and, thinking I would be viewed as if I was crazy, I hid them even more.

Even when we understand that the OCD is not who we are and is instead something we just have to deal with, we still don't feel as though people will understand. It is such a difficult thing to explain. The particular rituals and triggers can be very unique to each OCD sufferer so often it feels easier not to say anything at all, especially when trying to avoid the judgement and 'crazy' label. As an OCD sufferer I found that my biggest fear was to be looked at as if I was 'crazy', because I already had to fight that fear myself. This fear of misunderstanding keeps us from sharing or seeking help.

When OCD starts in childhood, I think for a range of reasons it is impossible to avoid thinking that you are crazy. The symptoms arrive and you think you're crazy. You hear about what OCD is (the false version) and so you still think you're crazy. You know your friends don't have it: therefore you must be crazy. Even if they have it, they are hiding it, so that doesn't make you any less crazy. But one of the most important things I have to say is:

*You. Are. Not. Crazy.* You suffer from a disorder and the disorder is *Not. Who. You. Are.*

## Misconception

The misconception around OCD is another reason why people find it hard to speak up about their struggle with OCD and seek help. It is truly why OCD is anxiety's *misunderstood* best friend. When people are asked if they know what OCD is, they will often tell you that it's that thing where people like to be clean and organised and put their pencils in a straight line. Although someone's compulsions *could* be to do with keeping things clean and orderly, this is not all there is to it, and the sufferer is not just organising for the sake of being organised. This *massive* misconception can stop people from potentially recognising that they themselves truly do have OCD. For me, OCD meant the opposite of being organised— and there came a time when OCD affected me in such a way that I couldn't even manage to put things away. This often meant I had an extremely messy room.

Growing up, that is exactly what I thought OCD was: cleanliness and organisation. This led to a longer road of figuring out that what I had was OCD, and a longer time of feeling like I was crazy. Once you find out what it actually is, you are amazed by how often you hear people claiming they have OCD because they like to keep their highlighters in a rainbow order or because they like to take neat school notes. Unfortunately, when you truly do have OCD, the misconception makes you feel like you can't tell anyone or seek help. You feel so ashamed of the way you are compelled to keep flicking a light switch on and off until you know your family's safe —and if you say 'I have OCD' people don't tend to think of it as a big deal because they simply think 'Oh, she's just anal about being tidy.'

One of the hardest parts of the misconception is that it has led to OCD being 'glamourised'. There is a famous quote from a reality television star that circles around social media. It goes along the lines of *People say OCD is a disease; I say it's a blessing*, and it features a woman who likes to organise her cookie jar a particular type of way. This false representation of OCD is painful to hear, when it can be so crippling and can cause the sufferer an immense amount of pain and emotional and mental distress.

## Highs and Lows

As my first two years of high school continued, I wore the heavy friendship necklace gifted to me by anxiety and OCD and continued to hide it as best I could from my friends and family. I felt as though I had somewhat of a grip on my depression and I went to school and played my sports just like many teenagers do.

I remember an exact moment in my life at this point. I was fourteen years old. It was the weekend and I was on the bus on my way to a friend's house. As I sat looking out of the window at the houses flashing by I remember having a conversation with myself saying, *That's enough, Sienna. It is time to stop the anxiety around Mum passing away. It is time to realise that she is going to be around for a long, long time and this type of anxiety and worry is only detrimental to your wellbeing.* I remember the exact street junction I was at when this happened. It was a big moment. I remember thinking that I could delay my worries until I was at least in my fifties, which was a much more ordinary time to expect to lose a parent. I sat there on the bus accepting this truth. It did not solve my OCD, but it was a truth I knew I needed to come to terms with and I worked hard to believe this was so.

Unfortunately, the following year I learned that no amount of compulsions and rituals could stop or undo what had happened when my biggest fear came true. I lost my mum to cancer.

In a matter of months, the one I trusted and loved the most in this world was gone. When she died, I felt a mixture of knowing deep down it wasn't my fault but also having some thoughts of: *Wait, was it?* And then in that vacuum of grief, the OCD gave me a new set of rituals to perform.

In this section, I want to share with you some of the highs and lows that I experienced whilst living with OCD and the exacerbation that comes with certain triggers, such as profound loss. Which is to say, life can throw some hard stuff at you sometimes. The hardest thing can be to learn that you have not caused it. Once my mum passed, the correlation between the intensity of the rituals and the stress and grief that I was enduring became apparent.

### The Mirror

This is the ritual that made my mother aware of my OCD after my crafty six or so years of being able to hide what I thought during this time was 'craziness'. This was before she got sick, and I was thirteen or fourteen. We had moved house again in my last months of primary school. I can't recall if my mum moved the mirror into the small hallway through which we entered the dining/kitchen/ living area or if I just had not noticed the mirror that much until my OCD decided that it was going to form my next ritual involving it. My OCD had now decided that whenever I passed a mirror I *had* to leave the mirror making sure I was looking at my teeth—and not just any tooth but the front right one, to be exact. This meant that every single time I passed this mirror I had to stop, because it is an extremely hard thing to do to pass a mirror quickly and look at the exact tooth you need to look at. Due to where this mirror was located I had to pass it *all. the. time.* Every time I wanted to leave my room and get something to eat or come out for dinner or do my chores or go to the lounge room or essentially go anywhere but the bathroom, then I had to pass this mirror. And alas, this mirror was not the bathroom mirror (in which I also had to do this ritual) but a very visible mirror. This initially led my mother and stepdad to believe I was a very full-of-herself adolescent who *wanted* to spend all day looking at herself in the mirror. Little did they know I wished for anything but having to look into a mirror, or even my reflection, as I also always had to do this ritual if I caught my reflection even in a window or kitchen appliance.

Soon, though, my mum picked up on the repetitive tendency and that this was not just a teenager checking herself out, and she put the dots together that it was a symptom of OCD and that I perhaps needed some help. Unfortunately, soon after was when my beautiful mother was diagnosed with cancer. She passed away nine months after her diagnosis and therefore I was unable to delve into the possible help I could have received with my trusted, safe place of a mother next to me to guide me through it. It is important to note that my OCD was discovered by my mum, not told to her. Because OCD is not something easily shared, and as discussed earlier, there are heavy feelings of shame and guilt associated with this disorder, my mother's starting the conversation made it a little easier to begin contemplating sharing this hidden aspect of my life. But then she was gone.

Twenty-seven days after my mum passed, I had my sixteenth birthday. It was a day I spent with my sister alone as we were still coming to terms with our new reality. I had not yet finished my third year of high school, and with two years still left to complete and a mother and home gone, my godparents took me in.

Without my beloved mother to guide me through what happened next, I was fortunate my godmother was there, even if she did not understand what was happening to me. I wish I could have had this book to give to my godmother during that time, because it would have made things easier for us all, and explained some of my unfathomable behaviour.

### The Bed and the Coathanger

This one sounds like a fairytale, doesn't it? However, it is anything but. This ritual was one of the hardest I have ever faced. It could relate to any type of putting away items, whether it was dishes, clothes, or even picking up and putting away groceries. The funny (but not actually funny) part of this ritual is that it completely goes against the misconception of OCD being something that super-tidy people have. The inability to put away items was truly crippling and time-consuming, and must have been very challenging for my godmother too. Putting items away became difficult, but putting clothes away—especially on coathangers—and making my bed became impossible.

During this period, my godmother was incredible. She did an exceptional job in simply being there for me with full support and no judgement even though OCD had a firm grip on me. Now I know that personal tragedies can make the OCD *a lot* worse. My OCD was so crippling during this time that the compulsions when putting my clothes away or trying to make my bed were so intense that I simply couldn't, and I *needed* my godmother to help me put my clothes away and make my bed, even though I was sixteen years old. The support my godmother gave me was crucial and I think that is important for parents who have a child with OCD in recognising and understanding that it is not laziness but a psychiatric disorder that can interrupt someone's ability to complete everyday tasks. For me, I *couldn't* put my clothes away. Whether it was in the drawer or placing the hanger down, I couldn't let go without making sure I was remembering a very specific memory of a good moment in my life. It had to be extremely specific and I had to be fully in that thought without the intrusion of any other thoughts (which is OCD's main characteristic), or I had to complete the compulsion of continuously re-putting away the clothes until it was completed properly.

During this period, I also struggled with putting the sheets on my bed. I had to do the exact same thought process when putting on each corner and it would often cause too much mental agony that I simply would avoid having to make my bed by going weeks without washing the sheets. This is where my godmother was able to step in and help with these tasks that had become near impossible for me to complete. Once I remastered the ability to make my own bed and put away clothes, it was much like the light switch and I felt immense relief that I could now accomplish these simple tasks without suffering.

## The Writing

This ritual made school extremely difficult and was more prevalent during my mum's sickness and especially after she passed away. My OCD would kick in when writing notes down in class or, worst of all, when I would have to write essays in exam conditions. So, when I was writing a certain word sometimes (when I say sometimes, I mean *a lot*) my OCD would kick in, and if I didn't finish off that word with a specific positive thought/memory perfectly as my pen left the page, then I would have to go back over that particular letter over and over until I had completed the compulsion correctly. Often I would have to retrace the letter exactly backwards of how I wrote it and then rewrite the letter again exactly how it was on top without my pen leaving the page and this could be repeated multiple times in one compulsion. Sometimes, I would be stuck holding my pen on the last point of the letter for minutes as I would be having such difficulty trying to finish the compulsion with the positive memory and I did not want to have to go back over my work as it would cause more distress. This compulsion included full stops and commas too (the OCD did not discriminate). This resulted in various holes of missing information in my school notes and missing chunks of lectures. There was one exam in year ten, after my mum had passed, where we were required to write five analytical essays in response to images we were given or passages of writing. My OCD kicked in so badly that I just had to completely skip one of the essays and not answer it. I remember the teacher asking me what happened when he gave my graded exam back, and of course I could not tell him that my OCD was so uncontrollable that I couldn't complete the exam, so I just gave a low, defeated *I don't know...*

Unfortunately, this compulsion soon made its way to my laptop. Even when typing on Word documents, if I did not click the key on the keypad with the correct positive memory then I would have to repeat the compulsion. Sometimes this meant my work would look like thisssssssssssssssssssssssss and eventually once the compulsion stopped I could backspace the extra letters. Or I would have to continuously press the key and backspace and press the key and backspace until the compulsion was correctly done. Sometimes it would result in me having to backspace until I felt okay as a form of 'retracing' the steps, because if I started fresh I wouldn't be stuck on that particular word. In fact, it was much like the walking ritual I described earlier. This last compulsion was the worst, as sometimes it made me delete paragraphs of work that I would have to rewrite, making it take much longer to complete my schoolwork.

### The Segments

Wow, this was a difficult one. This was also at the height of my OCD in the years after my mum had passed away. This was the one that made me just want to close my eyes and lie down on the floor because to have them open was too difficult. This ritual involved my OCD using the segments of the room where the wall meets the roof and the other walls, and the numbers had to correspond with the amount of times I would flick my vision from one segment to the other. It could mean from wall to wall or, if the roof was segmented, then segments of the roof and the walls (often from wall to roof in an upwards motion). The segments could even be the different areas between the ceiling fan blades. This could occur in any room I was in. Whether it was at home or at school or at a shopping centre, it didn't matter. It interfered with my ability to just do anything and my ability to just be, and it became especially prevalent at night as well due to the fact I would often be looking up at the ceiling. As with all the other rituals, it was a ritual caused by the compulsion to banish unwanted thoughts.

### The Bra

This one again was at the height of my OCD journey in the years after my mum had passed. It became mentally exhausting to simply get dressed. It was mostly when it came to my bra that the OCD would kick in. For those unfamiliar with the use of a bra, bear with me. When you go to put on a bra, some wearers often do up the clasp at the front and then turn the bra around to make things easier. This would be the exact moment that my OCD would kick in and I would have to do up and undo my bra countless times and turn it around and then turn it back around countless times. It would even happen when I was putting on my other clothes and had to step in and out of pants and put the t-shirt on and off and on and off—and so the simplest of tasks became mentally exhausting.

It was during that third year of high school with the death of my mum that I learned that, like many things in life, the journey with OCD has its ups and downs. The lows can be extremely difficult to deal with, but as I worked my way through my grief and anxiety there were also times where the OCD didn't completely consume me. I gradually learned that though there are tough times, it is possible to have your journey with OCD and enjoy life at the same time. It definitely takes time, but it is possible. I hope this can be a comforting thought if you are just embarking on your journey with OCD and after just reading all those super intense rituals.

I would consider the 'highs' of experiencing OCD to be a day or period of time that the unwanted thoughts occurred sparingly, resulting in minimal compulsions, and the 'lows' can be the points at which the OCD completely consumed me and even the act of just opening my eyes caused immense distress because it allowed more chances of compulsions. The timing of these highs and lows can vary throughout one's journey with OCD, however in my journey I have noticed certain external triggers can make the OCD more present. Thus far I have found these personal triggers to include my mum passing away, stress revolving around money and finances, stress revolving around school and academic performance (for example maintaining good grades, passing classes, and ultimately graduating high school and getting my degree) and stress revolving around sports injuries. The one thing most of these external factors have in common is a lack of control of the situation. And learning to accept a lack of control is an important part of the journey of healing, managing and recovering.

### Less Impactful Rituals

Not all OCD rituals completely consume you and they can often become a part of your daily routine. For example, I still brush my teeth a certain way and wash my body in the shower a certain way due to OCD, but the way in which I do these daily things does not have a major effect on my life, as long as they get done. However, in saying that, it is my experience that when you are at a major low point of your OCD—when your OCD is very high—then the rituals can become very present even in daily tasks that you already do a specific way, and they can make straightforward aspects of everyday living very difficult indeed.

When the OCD is not that bad, it does not *really* affect what I am doing but is still present—so it can be things with minor constraints such as when I want to read comments on social media posts, I have to read the top four and that's all. There are also things that I will do because of my OCD but I have been doing them for so long that for me it is my norm even if to others it would seem odd. For example, when reading (this is most common on social media) if there are repeated letters in a word such as 'youuuuuu' then I will need to count and see the amount of repeated letters that are used. The same thing happens if there are multiple exclamation points, full stops and commas. These are parts of my OCD that do not affect me negatively compared to other compulsions, unless my OCD is in hyper-drive and causes these things to become a repetitive compulsion on the same word or point of grammar.

### More Impactful Rituals

So there are times in my life when OCD has had a relatively lesser impact. But there are other times when there have been compulsions that have occurred when OCD has been at its most belligerent. This next part was very difficult for me to write out into words. Along with previously never wanting to have admitted to OCD, there are certain parts of OCD that I would never want to admit to or talk about because I understand that to others it sounds 'crazy'. For me, this includes these certain compulsions that I have had to do at my lowest points with OCD. These are the things I want to admit and tell you now, so that others do not feel alone.

The worst points of my OCD have been when the compulsions have had to be formed in the most physical and particular ways. The more particular a compulsion needs to be, the more difficult it is to perform right and therefore causes the make-up compulsions, repeat compulsions and retracing compulsions. Some physical traits have been to shake my head, firmly tap my head, or nod my head strongly backwards as if to get the unwanted thoughts out. Or to squint and display the revolt on my face in an expression to exhibit my disdain towards these thoughts. Another one is to jump, which is one that used to occur late at night as I tried to sleep. There was one compulsion that I remember clearly due to the distress that it caused me. This was once again during the height of my OCD and was severely particular. I had to:

- Jump a certain amount of times
- whilst looking at the roof (or sometimes eyes closed)
- with legs apart and not touching throughout the whole jump
- and landing slightly backwards from the take-off point
- without touching certain parts of the floor or any furniture
- without losing balance.

As you can imagine, this can be an extremely hard thing to execute all together, especially trying to keep balance with your eyes closed or being able to jump backwards whilst not touching any furniture in a confined space of a bedroom. If I missed any part of it, it caused me more distress and caused many 'retracing' compulsions to occur. I *had* to complete these compulsions to ensure that certain terrible things wouldn't happen and to get rid of the unwanted thoughts, to be able to get that relief at least for a moment, which meant I could finally sleep.

These immense lows and periods of jumping created even more difficulty when I severely injured my ankle playing soccer.

However, OCD still insisted that I had to jump. Even though it was a time where I wore a cast during the day and took it off to sleep and the doctors were considering surgery, I still had to do the compulsion which can show how strong these urges for relief are when suffering from OCD—and even though it hurt to do it! The pain of jumping with the severely injured ankle was less than the mental agony of resisting the OCD. (And yes, I tried with all of my being to have to *not* do the compulsions, however, it's not that simple when you have OCD and when you are at your most vulnerable. This is not something I am proud to admit, but it also goes to show how difficult and insistent OCD can be.)

## Relationships

It is not only the person suffering from OCD who can be affected by this disorder but also those around them. If you are the one that suffers from OCD, this is not for you to feel guilty about, because you have *nothing* to feel guilty about, but you can imagine that if OCD is having such a big impact on your life and wellbeing, then it is probably going to be affecting those around you too.

I have had some conversations with a mother whose child suffered from OCD. It came about out of nowhere when her daughter became a teenager as severe rituals suddenly appeared, crippling the life of her daughter. This young teen was unable to leave the house due to the severity of her OCD. With tears in her eyes, the mother confided in me how difficult and painful it was to watch her child suffer. She wished she could take away this pain, and she could tell when her daughter's suffering was at its most acute because in those times she was unable to hide her compulsions. Sometimes for those around the sufferer, it is only when OCD is at its most severe that the hiding becomes impossible and the compulsions visible to those around them.

For me, it was extremely hard when my OCD would require participation and cooperation involving another person. This happened a lot in the exacerbated periods of OCD after my mum had passed, and they often involved my godmother. It causes even more distress for the OCD sufferer because often they have to do their rituals perfectly to feel at ease, and when having to involve another person, the distress levels rise due to the fact that they want the other person to do their part perfectly, all the while continuing to hide the fact that they have OCD at all. This is a bit like the knocking on wood ritual. The one that involved my godmother was often when she would come to kiss me goodnight. If she was leaning over my bed to give me a kiss and a hug, I needed her to put her weight down perfectly in a certain way as she leaned over with her arms and as she got back up. I also *needed* her to then turn off and on the lights in a certain way, which I would hide by waiting for her to turn off the light and then say *Wait, stop* *wait for her to turn the light back on* and then make up something I had to say. It would also often involve the way she would close the door and the amount of times. Although I was feeling immense mental exhaustion, I know it would've been difficult for her as well. However, I was lucky that she just responded to my needs without judging me and allowed me to have some peace during this difficult time. For me, it was this open, non-judgemental mindset that helped me when things were at their worst. Even if we are not yet ready to discuss the disorder, not forcing this discussion and being patient is so important as well.

Another important point to touch on is that there can be a fine line between helping the OCD sufferer through a difficult compulsion, and enabling the OCD by doing what it wants. However, this is a very difficult line to find and it varies for every individual. Professional help can be needed in managing compulsions, and guiding all parties through.

For me now, I can find comfort in someone saying *I think that it is your OCD talking and not you?* and recognising that OCD has come for an unexpected visit and is affecting the way I behave. However, this is my own personal preference. To me, it is a comforting act that can have a grounding effect, and it is a simple reminder that the OCD is the OCD, and not me. This is also in parallel with being where I am now on my journey with OCD, and it requires the other person to be aware of my OCD and to know and understand what OCD is.

I have one more piece of advice: if you are someone who is close to someone that suffers from OCD or you are reading this and discovering that maybe you know someone who has OCD now that you know what it is: never joke about OCD by using the word 'crazy' or 'mad' or 'insane'. Most likely, the OCD sufferer is already facing that fear themselves and even if they do not seem perturbed externally, internally they may feel distressed, and hearing that word from others is only an additional burden. It is one thing for an OCD sufferer to use satire as a coping mechanism, and joke about being crazy, but having someone else say it to them is another thing entirely and it might validate their worst fear.

## Treatment

I wish OCD was something I didn't have to face and, ultimately, I know my life would be that much simpler without it, but I am just the one of many in the world who live with this disorder. In Australia, for instance, one in fifty people may suffer from OCD.[1] However, like many disorders, there is treatment out there to help you manage this most difficult of unwanted house guests, maybe even persuading them to take their stupid suitcase and go on a very long vacation rather than live right with you in the front room of your mind. The treatment can allow you to take a break and experience a reasonable degree of recovery. OCD need not be something that stops you from living a full life.

If you feel some recognition in my story, know you are not alone and it is okay to seek help. It is a very difficult thing to deal with alone—possible, but difficult. For me, my journey in being able to find help was interrupted by the death of my mum,

---

1. 'Obsessive compulsive disorder', SANE AUSTRALIA, sane.org/information-stories/facts-and-guides/obsessive-compulsive-disorder.

however that was the path I had already begun to go down with her. I understand it is extremely important to be able to seek help with someone you completely trust and feel safe with. Sometimes a person like your family doctor or a psychologist can take this role to help those around you understand what is going on. Earlier, I explained it was my mum who came to me about OCD, and her starting the conversation made it easier. Perhaps you want to start the conversation with a loved one but you are scared due to all the emotions that come with this disorder, so maybe it might help to give my story to that person you trust and they can start the conversation with you.

There are so many different ways in which you can receive help, and none of them means you are weak or vulnerable. Seeking help is a sign of strength and courage, and it actually means you are strong because you are taking that first step and standing up to your obnoxiously rude, insistent, mean, bossy, unwanted house guest. You might want to just feel the relief of opening up to someone about what you are going through, to have someone just listen and not talk. This might be a loved one or someone you don't know at all. Or you might want someone to talk to you about OCD to give you more information on the disorder without you having to talk at all. OCD thrives most when hidden from others, so taking this step can require enormous courage. You might just want someone to know you have it and understand the true complexities of it whilst you continue on your journey without judgement, like I had with my godmother. Or you might want to try and get involved with more intensive and extensive treatments that are available.

Where to begin? Whichever type of help you want to get, please know that it is out there and there are resources and people who can help and who want to help. The type of help you want to receive may change and differ over time. You might try something and that something is not for you, so you want to try something else—and that's okay. It happened for me as well. Getting help can feel hard and finding the right type of help that will support you can be a process, but it's important for you to feel supported with the help you are receiving. It can be a process because the type of help that works for some people might not work for you and vice versa. Luckily, there are lots of different types of help and there are people that will want to support you to help you find the right one that makes you feel comfortable and safe.

It can be uncomfortable and make you feel vulnerable in the beginning, but it is important to find help that is right for you and best for your overall wellbeing. In reading this, you might just be discovering that OCD is what you have been dealing with. Now you know it has a name, your first step may be that for now you just want to do more reading or research on it yourself before going down this path with anyone else—and that is okay too.

Below are a few ways in which I attempted to receive help, and what they meant for me. I share them so you can get some insight on what options are out there. Remember, this is simply what happened in my journey with OCD and does not mean it is what needs to happen with you on yours, as everyone's journey with OCD is unique to them. The first step is to know that there are professional healthcare people out there—GPs and therapists— who know how to help with OCD.

### Therapy

Therapy is a word that can comfort some people and fill others with dread. Some people swear by it and some people swear to it not working. At different times, I have felt both of these things. I think the important part to remember is that there is a relationship between the therapist and the patient. It might be easy to assume all therapists are the same because they have the same qualifications and so it does not really matter who is sitting across from you in the room. However, therapists vary greatly and a therapist who works for one may not work for another. For therapy to really work, there needs to be potential to establish a trusting relationship. There needs to be a feeling of support and non-judgement from the therapist to you, and for you to have a sense of respect for the therapist so you will actually listen, trust and take in what they are telling you, and this will also help you believe they are someone who is on your side.

In the beginning of high school, I was lucky enough to find an amazing therapist whom I trusted and respected and with whom I felt supported and not judged. This was before my mum had discovered my OCD, when she asked me to start seeing this therapist due to some separate family issues. In order to get to see this therapist, I first had to see the school counsellor. I did not feel those same feelings of trust and did not feel relaxed when having to have this appointment with the school counsellor and I already thought, *Oh no, this is not going to work when I have to see this therapist* ... But that just shows it is about the person and the relationship you have with that person. Just as in other parts of our lives, we do not all vibrate on the same frequency. You are not going to feel that immediate comfort—or potential for comfort—with certain people, and that is okay. In life we find our own people that we vibrate with and it needs to be the same for a therapist–patient relationship to work. Even though I was still scared and unsure in my first therapy session with the actual therapist, to my surprise this was someone I felt I could really trust and respect, and that they were genuinely invested in the person I was, not just the patient who was in front of them. They were someone I felt I would have been able to open up and talk to about my struggle with OCD but, unfortunately, they moved away just before my mum started to discover my OCD and before she got sick, so that relationship came to an end.

I saw another therapist once my mum got sick because my mum wanted to make sure my mental health was being taken care of at a time when she felt unable. I had made a deal with my mum that I would go, but I only went because of that deal with her and because I wanted to make her feel better. Unfortunately, the therapist I saw when my mum was ill was not for me. I dreaded these appointments and during them I felt uncomfortable. My anxiety would spike on the way to the therapist's office, during the appointment, and it would take some time after it was finished for my anxiety to come back down. This was a therapist who worked in the same centre as my former, trusted therapist but the experience was totally different because no two people are the same.

The main point when it comes to therapy is that you shouldn't have to settle with the first therapist you see. If the first therapist is someone you happen to hit it off with and you feel super comfortable and trusting with, then that is fantastic, but if you do not feel these things and it isn't just the first-time therapy nerves and you do not feel any future potential of comfort with this therapist, then it is completely okay to try again with someone else.

The first session with someone can always feel difficult because there are probably so many things that have happened in your life that you feel have shaped you and potentially caused OCD symptoms and anxiety, so you can't possibly think where you would start in trying to communicate to this stranger sitting across from you the extent of all these ins and outs of your life. However, it is that starting point that is the difficult part and once you're past it, things can start to be a lot easier if you feel you are with the right therapist.

My last point on therapy is that getting therapy does not mean you are weak. Seeking help is a sign of strength, as is accepting that help can make your life easier to live. Just as one goes to the doctor for a broken bone, it makes sense to seek help for a mental health challenge or disorder. It can feel more difficult, though, because it is 'all in your head'. And, it can be even more difficult because not everyone understands this. You wouldn't expect someone with a broken bone to continue on with life without help—and similarly, you do not have to continue life without help either, even if it's harder to take that first step. And the right type of help depends on the individual and their situation and needs.

## Medication

For some people, medication is an effective option. When my mum passed, I was diagnosed with chronic anxiety and acute depression and a recommendation was antidepressants, which the doctor informed me could potentially also help with my anxiety. This was at a point that my OCD was pretty much hidden to everyone except my godmother, and when talking to a doctor, I generalised it as anxiety. The doctor made it clear that there are many different types of antidepressant medication and the different dosage levels can also have different results. I only tried one type of antidepressant on different dosage levels however I felt no change or difference. If I had, perhaps I would have persisted. But it was not a course of action that felt right for me. It is important to note that psychopharmacology is a process and it is not uncommon for people to have to try several medications before finding the perfect match. As always, you should consult with your GP or psychiatrist who is trained in treating people with OCD as research shows the type of medication needed and dosage level differs for people with OCD.[2]

## Other Treatments

There are other treatments out there besides one-on-one therapy and medication. These are not ones I can give my personal experience on, but there are some I have heard amazing things about, even someone having near-eliminated their OCD symptoms. In particular, these include cognitive behavioural therapy and exposure and response prevention (ERP) therapy.

Cognitive behavioural therapy is a type of talk-therapy which focuses on reducing psychological distress through altering negative thoughts, behaviours, and emotional responses. It is different to other talk-therapies because it is very structured and it is based on the here and now of a patient's problems rather than trying to dissect the past. It is only intended to be a short-term treatment, used for months or even weeks but not years.

---

2. See iocdf.org/about-ocd/ocd-treatment/meds for the range of medications currently available.

ERP therapy is based on exposing the certain fears and triggers associated with OCD in a safe setting to help take away the power of these triggers and to help the sufferer learn that they can tolerate the discomfort of the obsessions without engaging in compulsions. The patient will be exposed to what triggers their OCD, for example, a light switch and are asked to not act out the compulsion. The therapist works with the sufferer and the trigger until they can tolerate the obsession without engaging in compulsions. It is a gradual therapy because the therapists are not trying to distress you—they want to help you and this has been a proven method.

Other treatments include support groups, aversion therapy, psycho-education, rational emotive behaviour therapy, psycho-therapy, systematic desensitisation, and group psychotherapy. I do not have experience with these therapies or know of a trusted source that has talked to me about them. But I am including them just to let you know that there are multiple options when trying to seek help for OCD, and if one type of treatment doesn't work for you then do not lose hope, as there are other options as well.

## Acceptance

One of the most important parts on my journey with OCD—from thinking I was crazy, to discovering the disorder, to living with the disorder—was finally accepting that I had it. Although discovering that you're *not* crazy and that you have a disorder brings a certain amount of relief, accepting that you *do* have a disorder is the next step—sometimes you can still feel just as crazy because it is called a 'disorder'. I fought this disorder for a long time through its most severe moments, slowly understanding and learning that what I have has a name. It wasn't until my first two years of university though that I did more research and learned how many people are really suffering from this disorder as well, and that there are others like me who also have to deal with compulsions and rituals. This information is something I wish I had access to as a child because that simple piece of knowledge would have brought me such relief much earlier, rather than having to wait until I was nineteen years old.

Although I can recognise that I had OCD since I was around eight and that it evolved and morphed with me as I aged, I can also recognise that I most severely suffered from the disorder once my mum passed and for the next five to six years it was at its worst. It was only after that time that I truly accepted the disorder, and understood that I needed to accept it in order to be able to move forward with my life and release some of the severe hold it had on me. It was causing me more distress to experience the OCD while actively trying to not accept that I had it. Acknowledging it would have removed a whole layer of difficulty in managing what I had. I understand that my response was due to a lack of awareness about the disorder and not understanding what I was dealing with. It is a big step to take, because OCD wants you to hide it in order for it to retain control but in accepting what you have, there is so much power—you arrive at the knowledge that you are an amazing, exceptional human being even with OCD.

Once I accepted that I had this disorder, I was able to take back some control. I was able to look at the disorder differently and understand that even though I had a disorder, it did not need to define me. The OCD is not who I am. I am who I am *despite* the OCD, and I now also understand and know that I am even more resilient and strong because of the OCD. I accept that I may have OCD but I am not going to wait until I can have a year without anxiety and its best friend unexpectedly showing up before I choose to enjoy my life. I am not going to try to instantaneously cure this disorder and cause myself more and more distress over its appearances and not allow myself to take peace in the easier days.

I have come to understand that making peace with OCD's unexpected arrivals and accepting its presence is truly important in feeling better and taking control. But I also know why arriving at this point of acceptance is part of a process. When first being introduced to this unwanted guest and experiencing its horrible company, your instinct is to fight it and somehow get it to leave you alone. However, this response only gives OCD more strength and allows it to plant its feet more firmly, basking in its ability to take all of your attention and focus. It revels in your stress.

But you see, there is a trick in beating this unwanted guest. It is in being aware of when OCD turns up and accepting its presence, but when it pulls out its suitcase primed and ready with bossy compulsions, then you call OCD out. Oh, how OCD hates to be named … You tell yourself that the compulsion you are being told to complete is just your bossy, mean OCD. And you don't fight anxiety's best friend to leave because that is exactly what it wants and it takes too much of your energy. You acknowledge its presence and allow it to stay quietly in the corner, but any time it reaches for the suitcase, you know to call it out. OCD is no more than an intrusive thought, feeling, sensation, image, or urge and you can learn to manage it in the way that you can learn to manage other thoughts, feelings, sensations, and urges.

I know this sounds a lot simpler than it is and to get to this point takes a lot of work, willpower and mindfulness. You accept that you have an unwanted house guest that loves to come and stay unexpectedly and you accept that it will try with all its might to impose its bossy nature upon you. But you also accept that OCD is not your heart, your soul, or your personality. Yes, you know that it will probably be back again but this is how you can learn to accept and have control over its presence and find some peace in knowing that eventually it will leave again.

It was not until I reached this kind of acceptance that I finally felt a level of peace. I understood that there may be some days (or weeks) in my life when OCD was going to kick my ass. But I was not going to let those difficult days (or weeks) ruin my whole life. I was going to enjoy my life in its entirety. I worked so hard on trying to just get rid of the whole disorder that it made it harder for me in the long run. At this point I could understand that I was not crazy and I was not alone. In this acceptance I found a level of control when OCD would make its presence felt. I could accept and understand and tell myself that I was experiencing a bout of OCD but that it did not need to define me. In some moments, if I recognised it as OCD, and that I was okay, sometimes (and I mean *sometimes*) it meant I didn't need to perform the ritual—but this was only possible after a lot of acceptance work. *Sometimes* is still something though, and I will take that as progress. This acceptance also sometimes allows me to pass through the OCD bouts with much more calmness and ease.

I understand that there are external factors that are huge triggers for OCD and these vary for each individual. I can't control these but accepting the disorder was a huge step for me and allowed me to reach the level of peace I have today.

## Success

As I look back, I know that, despite the pain and suffering I have experienced from this disorder, I have accomplished many things and some of these would have seemed at one stage impossible to me when I was at my lowest. It is so important to recognise your accomplishments no matter how big or small. This section is not here for me to brag about what I have achieved. It is here simply to share my accomplishments because I know that when you are severely suffering from OCD, it can feel nearly impossible to achieve anything, when the difficulty of completing even simple, daily tasks is too much. There have been many times throughout my journey with OCD when it has felt like all too much, and I want these words to offer light and hope to those who are in the same place as I was—and to know you can achieve so much even if you are experiencing the struggle of OCD. This part is something I wish my younger self could've known and understood.

Although I have OCD, I travelled to Singapore at the age of fifteen as part of a soccer team to represent my school in the Singa Cup, Asia's premier international youth tournament. Despite the severity of my OCD, I have graduated from high school, winning academic awards for my grades. I have worked nine jobs. I left

Australia at eighteen to play soccer and study at a university in the USA with a scholarship. I have gone on to achieve more athletic and academic scholarships, making it on the dean's list nearly every semester and becoming captain of my soccer team. I have graduated from university with honours with a Bachelor of Science in Business Administration majoring in Integrated Marketing Communications (specialising in Emerging Media). I am engaged to an amazing, supportive and loving man who accepts and understands me as I am. And, I am living my life with the least amount of OCD that I have ever experienced in the last sixteen years.

These next few things that I consider to be accomplishments might seem strange to someone without OCD but there have been times throughout my life when I couldn't do these things without being completely consumed by OCD, and which made these simple life pleasures not so simple at all ... Although I have OCD, I have also danced in the rain and laughed with glee. I have swum in the ocean at dusk and enjoyed delicious hot chocolate whilst appreciating a movie. I have gazed at the stars and the moon with a sense of abundance and wonder. I have maintained friendships and owned the power to cut off toxic ones. I have been a friend, a sister, a daughter, a granddaughter and an aunt. I have enjoyed deep conversations with friends about the universe at 3am and seen the sunrise over the horizon with hope and delight for the new day. These things represent success to me because when deeply suffering heavy bouts of OCD it can feel as though they are impossible. To simply live. To simply enjoy. To simply be ... without having the OCD in control.

For the parents or guardians of those with OCD, please understand that if a young person is in that heavy, severe part of their journey with OCD then be the patient, understanding person they need, because they have so much potential within them. They need to fight to overcome the hardest part of this battle they are facing first. Do not rush them, just support them and the healing and success will come as they find a way to manage the OCD rather than have it controlling them.

Success and OCD are not mutually exclusive and this is an important thing to know. You are so much more than your OCD and even if you are struggling right now and the OCD is weighing heavily upon you, I promise that there are better days ahead and a life that can be lived fully.

## Peace

As a sufferer of OCD, the one thing I longed for was peace. Maybe it is the same for you. The severe bouts can bring you mental exhaustion and pain unlike any other, but getting to a point in your life where you can truly say you have peace is a huge step. I am able to say that I have experienced peace though there were times when this seemed impossible.

Yes, I still face the odd bouts of OCD. Even as I wrote this piece, some bouts have come and gone. I still wash my body and brush my teeth a certain way due to OCD and I accept these as things that I can still do but which don't exhaust me. Sometimes I still can have some quite bad bouts. However, accepting that I have OCD started the healing process and allowed me to open up about the disorder to the ones I love. There will be difficult times and it will be rough but the healing can happen for a better life. I also understand and know that there are so many treatments that I haven't even tried yet, which also gives me hope to maybe one day eliminate the compulsions altogether. However, I know that I am strong enough to live my life fully and choose to enjoy all that my life has to offer, OCD and all.

If you are reading this and you also have OCD, I want you to read these next lines out loud to yourself.

I have OCD and therefore I am resilient.

I have OCD and I am also an exceptional, amazing, unique human being.

I have OCD and I can still achieve everything I want to achieve.

I have OCD and I choose to accept this to start my healing.

I have OCD but the OCD does not have me.

I am not my OCD.

I am not crazy.

I am not alone.

I am human.

And I am brilliant.

I hope my words help you know that you are not alone, and bring you some understanding or awareness of what is often hidden from view. And hopefully I have given you a bit more understanding about anxiety's misunderstood best friend.

For all of those dealing with OCD, I am sending you all my love and healing energy and I hope you are able to begin your journey to peace which I know you so long for. Know it is possible.

Peace is possible.

# Becoming, Part One, Two, Ad Infinitum

Katharine Pollock

*For my family*

When I was twenty-one, my brain broke. Although, the word 'broke' is inaccurate. After all, breaking implies a swiftness, a suddenness. My brain breakage happened gradually and intermittently, so perhaps it's more accurate to say my brain broke down, like a car on the side of the road. Over time, simple activities like showering, brushing teeth, walking, eating and drinking started to become Sisyphean struggles. Initially, I managed to keep what was happening inside my brain ... well, inside my brain. Before too long, I couldn't even control this. The first giveaway to my defective mind was the state of my bedroom.

In mentally sound times, I would arrange my wardrobe by colour and sleeve length, which some may say is not indicative of sound mental health. To which I retort, harumph! Since my brain had broken, however, my wardrobe had become a veritable floordrobe, with clothing strewn haphazardly across the floor. It was evidence of a morning ritual I had begun performing. You know, like an energising yoga flow or a grounding meditation. This was my special morning routine:

1.  Get dressed.
2.  Have an intrusive thought about sex or death so shocking and vile I would be immediately racked with guilt and self-loathing.
3.  Strip off.
4.  Get changed into a 'clean' outfit; one untarnished by said thought.
5.  Repeat process until the thought attached to the original outfit was magically erased.

On good days, I only had to change outfits two or four times (not three, because it had to be an even number. It also couldn't be six, as the number six was cursed, for some reason). On bad days it could get up to twenty. Once dressed and ready for work, I'd check eight times that the front door was locked, before walking up and down the front steps ten times, and retracing my steps to the bus stop a further twelve times. Thankfully we had paper tickets back then and I didn't have to tap a card on a sensor twenty times during peak hour.

I'd been experiencing intrusive thoughts with increasing frequency and severity, each one causing extreme mental anguish. If you're not someone who's had OCD, you might be thinking that intrusive thoughts are no big deal. Everybody has them once in a while: it's par for the course of being walking, talking meat sacks. I mean, who hasn't thought, *par exemple, Imagine if I pulled my pants down, right here, right now, in front of my grandmother's open casket?*

The difference between those with OCD and those without is that most people without OCD are capable of rationalising the intrusive thought away as just a misfiring electrochemical signal. In an age of Pornhub and *The Human Centipede*, it's no wonder we occasionally think depraved or taboo things. As a person with OCD, however, I would be deceived by the thoughts. I was terrified that the irrepressible perverse and violent thoughts were actually latent desires. Sometimes I might be cogent enough to recognise this wasn't actually the case, but the guilt and shame over the thoughts would still be debilitating.

I started to become petrified that those around me knew what I was thinking. I was convinced that it was written all over my face, and I worried that I'd somehow let slip an evil thought when chatting to a friend or composing an innocuous text message. I also smoked a bit of weed from time to time in an effort to calm my frayed nerves. I stopped after I became convinced that I actually was speaking my secret deviant thoughts aloud: as if the usual side effects of weed aren't bad enough. That being said, I felt increasingly paranoid and low-key delusional even when I wasn't high, so it wasn't too drastic a change, really.

It was becoming increasingly difficult for me to concentrate at work or to perform menial tasks with even a modicum of concentration. The elephant in the room was making too much noise for me to hear anything else but its stomping footsteps. Just about the only thing I could do to take my mind off my mind was to watch TV. Specifically, *Buffy the Vampire Slayer*. I would perch on the windowsill, smoking and ashing out the window, with one foot balanced on the armrest of the couch and one eye fixed on the television. I'd seen *Buffy* all the way through enough times that I could easily catch up on the show if I got caught up in my thoughts. Not to mention that research has shown that in periods of high stress, returning to something familiar can provide comfort, in large part because we know how the thing we're watching will resolve.[1]

*Buffy* came out in 1997, when I was in grade four. It was far too grown-up and scary for my tender years, but I snuck a peek whenever my parents weren't looking. I was too young to appreciate the more mature thematic elements, but the spooky-ooky vampires thrilled me. Also, Xander Harris gave me funny feelings. In my early thirties, not a lot has changed, except that I now realise Xander is the textbook personification of toxic masculinity and quite possibly a self-insert character for the show's thoroughly dubious creator Joss Whedon.[2] But that's a dissertation for another day. I wanted to *be* the eponymous heroine, Buffy Summers. She was fierce, strong, independent and had a bomb wardrobe.

In my maturing years, I've come to embrace my true nature as a Willow Rosenberg. Well, if we're being pedantic, I'm really a Willow sun with a Buffy moon and a Cordelia Chase rising. *Buffy* was comforting to me not just because it was familiar, or because

1. 'Press play: The link between stress and re-watching the same TV show on repeat'. *this.*, Deakin University, this.deakin.edu.au/self-improvement/link-between-stress-watching-tv.

2. Zenobia Frost, et al., 'Was Joss Whedon the real big bad of "Buffy"?'. *Junkee*, 18 February 2021, junkee.com/joss-whedon-buffy-season-6/288107.

I could effortlessly zone out to the bright colours, chunky shoes and spunky vernacular, but also because it was aspirational. If Buffy and the Scoobies (the moniker given to Buffy and her closest friends) could survive multiple apocalypses, surely I could withstand my own malfunctioning synapses. *Buffy* is also famously allegorical, using vampires and demons to symbolise identity, heartbreak, sexuality and addiction.[3]

I hadn't yet named my disorder—I didn't yet know what I had—but I knew something was very wrong, and that I felt very alone. Too ashamed and confused to vocalise what I was going through with my friends or family just yet, I instead turned to popular culture. I have always found solace in pop culture, whether it's film, TV, books, comics or music. I've worked in record shops and bookshops, attended comic conventions and trivia nights, and sat through nine-hour movie marathons. I firmly believe that the distinction between so-called high and low culture is arbitrary, snooty and fundamentally misogynistic, and I view the world through a bricolage of characters, songs and images.

When I tried to find evidence of people going through whatever it was I was going through, however, I was met with a dearth of realistic representations. Pop culture has by and large portrayed OCD as being little more than fastidiousness, maybe a little harmless germaphobia. Depictions of characters in film and TV who have OCD or what could be something akin to it are few and far between, but notable mentions are television's Adrian Monk from *Monk*, who has pathological germaphobia, and Monica Geller from *Friends*, a highly strung neat freak. The list of celebrities who have OCD is more extensive. However, discerning who has diagnosed OCD as opposed to merely compulsive tendencies is up for debate. The list of celebrities who have either acknowledged having it outright, hinted at it or merely been the subject of speculation includes David Beckham, Justin Timberlake, Frank Sinatra, Howard Stern, Howie Mandel,

3. Douglas Kellner, '*Buffy, the Vampire Slayer* as spectacular allegory: A diagnostic critique'. UCLA, pages.gseis.ucla.edu/faculty/kellner/essays/buffy.pdf.

Howard Hughes, Megan Fox, Fiona Apple, Charlize Theron, Billy Bob Thornton, Jessica Alba and David Sedaris. My only takeaway from the eclectic collection of names is maybe don't call your child Howard: evidently, it's cursed. By and large, however, discussion and depictions of OCD in pop culture is confined to harmless displays of quirky eccentricity. This may not seem significant depending on how much stock you put in pop culture, but we know from discussions of race and gender that underrepresentation and misrepresentation in media perpetuates stigmatisation and marginalisation.[4] If a person cannot see themselves reflected on screen, they inevitably start to feel … well, not unlike a vampire unable to cast a reflection in the mirror.

Apart from Buffy flippantly describing watcher and school librarian Giles as being obsessive compulsive,[5] Buffy never actually directly tackles OCD. However, it does depict equivalent and interrelated issues such as PTSD, grief, loneliness, anxiety and existential dread. I also don't think it's too much of a stretch to suggest that at its core—its Hellmouth, if you will—the Buffyverse is all about control. And what have we started to learn about OCD today, boys and gals and non-binary pals? It all hinges on control. Allusions to control—characters' attempts to exercise control, and their many and varied failures to actually do so—are implicitly and explicitly peppered throughout the show's seven seasons. Take Buffy's watcher Giles telling Wesley (also Buffy's watcher, and Faith's, who is also a Slayer … maybe let's not go deep into the character profiles here) that controlled circumstances are non-existent in Sunnydale.[6] Or when Buffy's best friend Willow says to

4. Hannah Ajala, 'Why is proper representation on TV important for diversity?'. *Media Diversity Institute*, 28 April 2021, media-diversity.org/why-is-proper-representation-on-tv-is-important-for-diversity.

5. Season 2, episode 13, 'Surprise', *Buffy the Vampire Slayer [BtVS]*, written by Marti Noxon, directed by Michael Lange, 1998.

6. Season 3, episode 14, 'Bad Girls', *BtVS*, written by Doug Petrie, directed by Michael Lange, 1999.

Buffy that witchcraft is fundamentally all about control.[7] And one more, when Xander urges Buffy not to let her fears control her.[8] Buffy tries to fight back hordes of vamps throughout the seasons, but they keep coming. Giles tries to protect Buffy, but—spoiler alert—she dies, twice. Xander tries to make Buffy fall for him, but because she's a human, not an automaton, she doesn't. Willow's character arc, in particular, is all about control. She's a girl who wants to loosen the reins on her rigid life, but finds it difficult to muster up the courage to do so, insisting that she is incapable of acting spontaneously, lest she appear awkward or clumsy.[9] Willow's fear of losing control was so analogous to me it was uncanny. Even more uncanny than Willow coming face to face with her vampire doppelgänger (if you know, you know).[10]

I have always put a primacy on control, whether it's regulatory control of my emotions, control over what and how much I eat, control over how others see me, or control over my academic and professional outputs. It's taken until this point in my life to accept that control cannot be maintained, at least not forever. You can only grip onto something for so long before your muscles cramp or your palms get sweaty. As Willow's werewolf boyfriend Oz describes in season eight (yeah, yeah, it's the comic book continuation, but it's still canonical), spells are all about the manipulation of energy, in which magic wielders (or users, to align with the addiction motif running throughout the show) compress energy so tightly that it eventually, inevitably, explodes.[11] Try as I might, I couldn't control the onslaught of thoughts or their associated compulsions.

---

7. Season 3, episode 16, 'Doppelgängland', *BtVS*, written and directed by Joss Whedon, 1999.

8. Season 4, episode 1, 'The Freshman', *BtVS*, written and directed by Joss Whedon, 1999.

9. Season 2, episode 6, 'Halloween', *BtVS*, written by Joss Whedon and Carl Ellsworth, directed by Bruce Seth Green, 1997.

10. Season 3, episode 16, 'Doppelgängland', *BtVS*, written and directed by Joss Whedon, 1999.

11. Jane Espenson, *Retreat*. Dark Horse Comics, 2009.

And it wasn't long before I exploded. I hit rock-bottom only a few months after my OCD first flared up. Well, more precisely I hit the bottom of the bathtub, while stepping in and out of the slippery tub in a frantic attempt to undo a thought. The next day, at my parents' house, I sat down at the breakfast table with a fried egg in front of me and an egg-sized lump on my forehead, and I took a deep breath.

'Mum, Dad, I think something's wrong with me. I can't stop thinking bad things. I can't stop … touching things.'

After quickly clarifying that I wasn't confessing to masturbating (no shame in the game, just not the most pertinent disclosure at that time), I shared the rest. I neglected to reveal the specific details of the 'bad things' I thought about, but I explained the compulsions and ruminations. I didn't name what I had as OCD at that point, because I didn't know—or I didn't want to know— what I had. I was terrified to admit something was wrong, because if I admitted something was wrong it meant that something was really wrong. Try saying that five times fast (and if you'd like an intermediate exercise, try it while simultaneously checking the stove is off eighteen times).

As scared as I was, the fear of whatever was happening to me continuing or getting worse was far scarier. The shame I was feeling was even worse than the fear. This is something that comedian and writer Rachel Bloom writes about eloquently and candidly. Bloom is one of the few famous people I've discovered who discusses her experiences with OCD with full transparency, although she is quick to clarify that she is not entirely sure if the condition she had was technically OCD, or just a convenient diagnosis.[12] Despite her prefacing statement, she describes a formative experience that would resonate with anyone with OCD. Remembering an occasion when she was on the toilet as a child, Bloom writes that she felt compelled to touch her finger to a piece of toilet paper she

12. Rachel Bloom, 'Okay, now I'll talk about the OCD thing'. *Glamour*.

13. November 2020, glamour.com/story/rachel-bloom-okay-ill-talk-about-the-ocd-thing.

had used to wipe herself, before putting that finger in her mouth. She immediately rinsed out her mouth but was utterly overcome with shame.[13] What Bloom manages to do in her admission is to articulate the trifold mental, emotional and bodily reaction to an OCD trigger. It's so overwhelming that it really does necessitate all caps, as Bloom uses in her writing, to convey how it feels. It's not just shame. It's SHAME. Bloom goes on to describe the terrible isolation that OCD can induce. She writes that while she does not really want the label of obsessive compulsive disorder, she found solace in feeling less alone once she had a name for what she was experiencing.[14]

After I told my parents what was happening to me, they promptly took me to see my family GP. They drove me there and sat with me in the room as though I was still a child, but I didn't mind. I didn't want to be any more alone than I already was.

In the doctor's office, I once more described what I was going through—the counting, the checking, the paralysing terror, the SHAME—and in return my doctor gave me something more valuable than a referral to see a shrink or a script for anti-depressants, both of which she also provided. She named it. *Obsessive Compulsive Disorder.* As though the SSRIs she prescribed had already kicked in, having a name for my disorder prompted immediate and tangible relief. I felt less alone, as though the other people around the world grappling with OCD were all in the room with me. She proceeded to tell me that I was concurrently experiencing a mental breakdown, brought on from the unmanageable cognitive load of OCD. This, too, was oddly nice to hear. Ah, I thought, in a slightly dissociated way, my thoughts still swirling chaotically with macabre and perverse disturbances. *My brain has just ... crumbled, like feta cheese.*

---

13. Ibid.

14. Rachel Bloom, 'Okay, now I'll talk about the OCD thing'. *Glamour.* 13 November 2020, glamour.com/story/rachel-bloom-okay-ill-talk-about-the-ocd-thing.

The psychologist she referred me to was an easygoing, middle-aged woman with neat brown hair. We clicked, and I retained her services for nine years thereafter before moving interstate and finding someone else. She operated out of a shared clinic with beige carpeting, off-white walls and khaki-brown furniture. The only splash of colour was the abstract blue-and-green wall art and the odd ocean landscape. The incongruousness of the bright colours failed to enliven the drab room, instead lending the impression the art was direct from an IKEA showroom. I suppose it was all deliberate, the autumnal tones suggesting neutrality and the aqua hues connoting serenity. Look at me, reflectively psychoanalysing the colour scheme: I guess it goes without saying that I've had years of intensive therapy.

My shrink—I'll call her Sharon—had a light-touch approach to our sessions. She'd make me a cup of weak, milky tea before sitting down in front of me with a pen and pad, listening and taking notes. Occasionally she'd interrupt to clarify something I'd said, or to give me some insight into my behaviours. At the end of each session she'd give me homework in the form of cognitive behavioural therapy exercises. CBT, if you don't already know, basically intends to disrupt cognitive distortions: to challenge unconscious and conscious beliefs and attitudes, and ultimately to change thought patterns and behaviour. To this end, Sharon had me do things such as dysfunctional thought journaling (noting down when I had an intrusive thought, what triggered it, the intensity of the distress it caused, and my reaction to it). I neglected to write down the more intense thoughts. After all, I didn't want her to think I was crazy or, worse, unlikeable! (I'm joking. Kind of.) I also did progressive muscle relaxation, deep breathing and ABC functional analysis, which stands for antecedent-behaviour-consequence and interrogates what preceded and proceeded an event, as well as the event itself.

If all of this is a bit acronym-heavy, I feel you. When I started to fizzle out from all the analysis and abbreviation, she would have me close my eyes and picture myself on a canoe floating downstream. On the shore, or perhaps even swimming towards me, was a monster, which represented an intrusive thought. She would have me invite it to approach, thus challenging me to take the scenario to its worst possible outcome. It was meant to prove that nothing bad could actually eventuate from letting the monster get close, but I'd seen 'Nightmares',[15] the episode of *Buffy* in which the characters' nightmares become reality, and 'Fear, Itself' in which, well, the same thing occurs, too many times.[16] I now firmly believed that just because it was in your head was no guarantee it couldn't hurt you. As Xander opines, simply closing one's eyes doesn't make these things go away. Suffice to say, I often proved too obstinate to tackle an exercise like ABC, and so Sharon would patiently listen as I spoke about, just for instance, my love of *Buffy* for the entirety of a session. Initially, while my medication kicked in and I came to grips with the realities of my disorder, I found my sessions difficult. It was only through time and practice that I was able to commit to the work of getting better.

Shortly after embarking on therapy, but still not out of the woods, my older brother called me. My mum had brought him up to speed on my feta-cheese brain and he was calling to offer me his support. It was demonstrable proof, as if I needed it, of my family's unconditional love. It was also one of my lowest points. I was smoking (I only smoked for about three months, stopping after anxiety over lung cancer surpassed the temporary relief smoking gave me from my more generalised anxiety) and I started grinding the cigarette into the side of my chair, once, twice, eighteen times over. I couldn't hear what he was saying, like there was poor reception, except the interference was coming from inside my brain. I was consumed with intrusive thoughts. Just by the by, intrusive is an insufficient word, if you ask me. It sounds more

---

15. Season 1, episode 10, 'Nightmares', *BtVS*, written by David Greenwalt and Jos Whedon, directed by Bruce Seth Green, 1997.

16. Season 4, episode 4, 'Fear, Itself', *BtVS*, written by David Fury, directed by Tucker Gates, 1999.

like a nosy neighbour than an irrepressible thought about, for instance, X-rated sex or unconscionable violence. Linguistics aside, thankfully my brother ended the phone call before I resorted to putting the butt out on my wrist just to silence the thoughts. I relit my cigarette and stared out at the dark sky, trying to envision myself safely in the canoe. But I was capsized, the monster had a hairy, gnarled claw around my ankle and it was pulling me under.

Another symptom I experienced was the unshakeable conviction that my friends and family were going to die. Not in their ripe old ages, but right now, and directly because of me. As an atheist, I managed to be persuaded by some very superstitious thinking in this area. I was convinced that my thoughts had the power to cause car crashes or heart attacks. I had to turn light switches on and off, or touch my tongue to the roof of my mouth at precisely the right angle twenty times while counting down from one hundred in order to undo a thought, thus miraculously staving off imminent death. I hated when my housemates or boyfriend would leave the relative safety of the house, and I would repeatedly urge them to stay safe. I thought that if I didn't tell them out loud and often, they would die. I was hopping, skipping and jumping over cracks to avoid breaking everyone's backs. And did I get so much as a thank you?

When I look back, it's remarkable that I was able to maintain living in a share house and having a boyfriend for as long as I did. My housemates were actually resoundingly supportive, if often bewildered and occasionally frustrated. I tried to hide my compulsive actions from them, but turning light switches on and off repeatedly is pretty difficult to cover up. Noticing that my knuckles were cracking and bleeding from washing my hands, one of my housemates stuck a picture of a muscular hunk above the bathroom sink, with a speech bubble coming out of his mouth reading, 'Do you really need to soap up? Just chill!' Another of my housemates would sit and listen to me as I spoke through and around the issues plaguing me—not offering a solution, just a shoulder.

As things were getting really hairy, my boyfriend at the time broke up with me. As I tied and retied my high top Chuck Taylors, he muttered, 'I can't deal with this,' and walked out the front door. As he left, I called out plaintively, 'Stay safe.' I hated myself for voicing the desperate platitude, considering he'd coldly dumped me for excessive shoe lacing mere seconds before, but I worried if I didn't vocalise it, he'd surely die. I didn't want that on my already overburdened conscience. Looking back, I don't blame him for splitting up with me. We'd only been together for a few months, and we were young and naïve. Not to mention that lacing high tops takes a long time. Maybe if I'd worn low top Converse we'd have had a chance. But as it stood, it was all too intense for him. We managed to stay together for about six months. If he'd known the real content of my thoughts, he probably would have bolted far sooner.

Apart from Rachel Bloom, one of the very few celebrities to openly discuss their condition in a way that resonates with the more confronting aspects of my own experience is Lena Dunham. She writes not just about the outward-facing elements of her condition, but also what it looked like *inside* her brain when she was at her worst. In a piece written for the *New Yorker*, recounting her childhood spent in therapy she discloses that she was a highly phobic, anxious child and teenager.[17] Elsewhere in the piece, she recalls her thrice-weekly sessions, writing that while the therapy helped, it could not prevent the consuming fear and anxiety she was increasingly feeling. She discloses that she would force herself to envision her parents having sex, as a way to block out the other thoughts and images that would spontaneously enter her brain. In a specific detail which would ring true to anyone with OCD, she adds that she would summon the image of her parents engaging in intercourse in sets of eight.[18]

---

17. Lena Dunham, 'Difficult girl'. *The New Yorker*, 25 August 2014, newyorker.com/magazine/2014/09/01/difficult-girl.
18. Ibid.

Dunham is equally candid about OCD when depicting the dangerous, violating or humiliating aspects of the condition in her TV series *Girls*. Protagonist Hannah Horvath is shown onscreen powerlessly obeying the compulsion to insert a cotton bud so deeply into her inner ear that she damages her ear canal.[19] Loath as I ever am to impose an autographical reading on a text (hello, historical diminishment of women's art as 'merely' autobiographical), Hannah's experience very closely mirrors that of Dunham, right down to eight being the magic number. Hannah confesses to experiencing the urge to envision a murder eight consecutive times, and to having to masturbate eight times a night as a pre-teen. Her shocking admissions are a call back to season one when, during a fight with Hannah, her friend Marnie yells that she would never betray Hannah's secret: excessive masturbation enacted in order to prevent physical and mental disease and deterioration.[20]

Dunham's discussion of her personal struggles with OCD, as well as her on-screen representations, boldly illuminate an element of OCD which is usually unacknowledged in film and television. Maybe because it doesn't map neatly onto depictions of manic pixie dream-girls enacting whatever harmless quirk they're invested in, to be portrayed as 'kooky cute'. Less 'kooky cute' is the harsh reality of intrusive thoughts and the magical thinking that drives compulsions. Sufferers of OCD enact compulsions to negate their distress and to prevent negative outcomes from transpiring, but of course, compulsions actually exacerbate the intrusive thoughts, making them more persistent and more distressing. And yet, even if we're armed with this knowledge, people with OCD can rarely resist the urge to obey the compulsion. Despite undeniable logic, not to mention risk of public humiliation, severe wax blockage and inner-ear bleeding, we're compelled to drive figurative—or literal—Q-tips deep into our ears. Over and over again.

---

19. Season 2, episode 8, 'It's back', *Girls*, written by Lena Dunham, Steven Rubinshteyn and Deborah Schoeneman, directed by Jesse Peretz, 2013.

20. Season 1, episode 9, 'Leave Me Alone', *Girls*, written by Lena Dunham, Bruce Eric Kaplan and Deborah Schoeneman, directed by Richard Shephard, 2012.

Some individuals with OCD actually are more of the Adrian Monk or Monica Geller variety, largely experiencing things such as germaphobia, hand-washing, checking behaviours and contamination fear, all of which can be equally severe. I can only speak from my experience as someone whose OCD revolved around nasty, naughty thoughts. Intrusive thoughts of the taboo variety usually concern the fear of doing something immoral or inappropriate, and generally reflect one or more of four societal taboos: aggression and violence, religious or moral scrupulosity, sexual deviance or unwanted sex acts, and health anxiety.[21] Compulsions can be less visible, such as mental ruminations and reassurance-seeking, but can also include retracing steps, washing hands and performing elaborate checking rituals.

A blog post on PsychCentral handily provides, as an example of an intrusive thought, the urge to yell offensive words in church. Likewise, they provide as an example of a compulsion the impulse to recount seventy-seven Hail Marys in order to erase the urge.[22] I find this very funny, but then, as an atheist, I never experienced the sacrilegious variant of OCD. *Ba-dun-tish*. Meanwhile, a quick glance on Reddit shows that copromania, or obsession with faecal matter, is a persistent theme, with one post titled 'Fear of farting',[23] and another, 'Does anyone else have poop obsession?'[24] I can relate to both of these, but then as someone who is both a *Pink Flamingos* fan and has recurrent digestive issues, that's perhaps to be expected. Maybe you, the reader, find the idea of a faecal fixation funny, proving that OCD really *does* have something for everyone.

---

21. 'Taboo OCD types'. New England OCD Institute, www.ocdtypes.com/taboo-ocd-types.php.
22. Arash Emamsadeh, 'OCD and the need to be in control'. PsychCentral, 14 December 2018, psychcentral.com/blog/fearless/2018/12/ocd-and-the-need-to-be-in-control#4.
23. 'Fear of farting'. Reddit, reddit.com/r/OCD/comments/7pi3hj/fear_of_farting.
24. 'Does anyone else have poop obsession?'. Reddit, reddit.com/r/OCD/comments/1nodax/does_anyone_else_have_poop_obsession.

*record scratch* *freeze frame* You're probably wondering how I got in this situation. How does a person go from not thinking about such things as poop, sex and murder all the time, to thinking about it all the time *plus* unpaid overtime? By my own estimation, the causation of all of this is partly nature, partly nurture and partly pot luck. But for the sake of the narrative, I'll start with nurture. My recollections are mine alone: I don't wish to impose judgement, shame, or blame on anybody whom I love. While formative experiences inevitably plant seeds for our development, I maintain that it is love which ultimately shapes who we become. I was raised with unconditional love, and this is the true legacy of my family. With that (dutifully but, I believe, crucially) acknowledged, it's my perception that various members of my family have long-navigated their own relationships with anxiety. My childhood was lovely and contended—just very safe. I see this as a reaction to a fear of the unknown and unknowable. If something was challenging or frightening it was strategically avoided or delegated to somebody more immediately competent to take care of. This was an outward expression of love: *I love you, so I will do the difficult thing for you.* Or, *I love you, so I won't expose you to the scary thing.* I truly appreciate the sentiment, but I also recognise that it may have fostered in me an unwillingness to challenge myself or to confront unpalatable realities.

Perhaps unsurprisingly, coming from this environment, I wasn't an especially athletic child. Outsiders often assumed I would be a sporty kid, based entirely on my long, skinny limbs, but my constitution was basically that of Linton in *Wuthering Heights*: pasty and frail.[25] Physical activities I failed to master include but are not limited to: skipping with a rope, diving (not to be conflated with belly-flopping, of which I was, and remain, a master) and riding a bike. I was largely uninterested in anything that could be even loosely described as outdoorsy, and in phys. ed. tried my best to get out of everything. As far as my PE teacher knew, I had a continual heavy flow from ages twelve to seventeen,

25. Emily Brontë, *Wuthering Heights*. Penguin Books, 2003.

and the poolside bleachers got intimately acquainted with my rear end. If I couldn't actually get out of an activity, I would minimally exert myself, even conspiring to read a copy of *Where's Wally* while unhurriedly walking the mandatory yearly school marathon. Likewise, I made a concerted effort to avoid maths and science, choosing to doodle in my margins through class and putting in negligible effort during exams.

It may seem contradictory, then, to reveal that I was a bookish kid. I loved English, and was a voracious reader, entering the MS Readathon every year and hoovering up books at the Scholastic Book Fair. In year seven, I attended a sleepaway camp for aspiring young writers. I don't recall exactly what I wrote about, but I do remember using the word 'resplendent' far too many times in a short story. I would use multisyllabic words which did not make a scrap of contextual sense in games of make-believe with my friends, just to impress them with my expansive vocab. Later, in high school, I voluntarily joined the circuit debating squad, and enrolled in English Extension. This is another reason why I related so much to Willow, who in *Buffy* season one is a mousy, nerdy girl with low self-confidence and a wardrobe picked out for her by her mother. Check, check and check. However, unlike Willow, my book smarts only extended to books, as in novels. I wasn't automatically good at maths, science or sport, so I didn't put in the effort. My logic was that if I didn't try and I failed, it was controlled, predetermined failure. If I put in the effort and I still failed, I was a failure.

I went to university straight after high school, expecting it to be easy-breezy and liberating. I foresaw myself reading in a labyrinthine library underneath the warm glow of a green banker's lamp. In my fantasy, my studious reverie would be interrupted by a tap on the shoulder, delivered by one of my many hip, bohemian friends. They would invite me to the campus café, where we would drink bottomless coffee, and later, beer, without ever getting too jittery or too drunk. Afternoons would be spent lazing on the lawn or protesting something or other on the forecourt. At night,

I would hold court with sophisticated conversation at parties, or perform endearingly tone-deaf karaoke at the campus bar. I would of course graduate top of the class without any difficulty at all, and each one of my lecturers and tutors would quietly weep during my graduation ceremony. *Maybe* there would be a standing ovation. I would be just like Rory in *Gilmore Girls* or Joey in *Dawson's Creek*. I conveniently forgot that each character had bouts of anxiety in their college years, because it didn't fit with my fantasy.

In reality, I went from my small private high school with a student body of five hundred to a sprawling university where I was frequently lost. I made very few friends and suffered from crippling imposter syndrome. Buffy has a similar crisis of confidence when she goes to college, admitting that she sometimes still wants to lug around a security blanket.[26] In a bid to get her out of her funk, Xander tells Buffy that whenever he is feeling at a loose end, he asks himself what Buffy would do. Unfortunately, I didn't think to call on this particular episode at the time, so I remained utterly at sea.

My feelings of disorientation and dissatisfaction extended beyond my tertiary troubles when I started dating a boy who turned out to be a walking, talking regulatory body. Teetotalling and supercilious, he frowned upon drinking or socialising, and didn't like me doing anything he hadn't explicitly approved of. All of which is a nice way of saying he was emotionally abusive and, in general, a total drag. For the nearly three years we were together, I became progressively isolated from my friends and from any sense of self-worth or autonomy. Suffice to say, I did not have the hedonistic or life-affirming college experience I'd expected. I didn't confide in anybody about anything I was experiencing, because—are we sensing a parallel here?—I didn't want to admit even to myself that anything was wrong.

Towards the end of the relationship, I moved out of my parents' house and into a share house. My boyfriend had not pre-approved my decision and was predictably irate. One night, my housemates

---

26. Season 4, episode 1, *BtVS*, 'The Freshman', written and directed by Joss Whedon, 1999.

were out partying while I dutifully stayed at home. They happened to meet my boyfriend's friend, who revealed that my boyfriend was dating somebody who definitely wasn't me. Apparently, he'd been seeing her since the night one year ago when he'd broken up with me, before changing his mind the next day. After they told me, I mustered up the scrap of dignity I had left and broke up with *him*.

I pretended I was okay about all of this, but the cumulative effect of the three years had destabilised me, as though the axial tilt of my planetary body had shifted. Still, shortly thereafter, I started dating another boy, and I caught up on all the things I'd been missing out on. Insert obligatory montage of me drinking and partying, deferring from uni, working full-time at my weekend record shop job, subsisting on packet mie goreng, breaking up with my new beau, getting back together, and breaking up once more over excessive shoe lacing. And yes, the maths on that is four break-ups between two relationships. During this time I also had an obligatory one-night stand (which was as good as sex with a straight man who believes condoms are optional can be), a close friend fell over backwards into oncoming traffic, remaining comatose for months, and *The X Files: I Want to Believe* standalone film was released. Despite all of these varying horrors, the world continued turning. But *my* world was spinning too quickly.

I mention all of these formative events in an attempt to elucidate the context around my eventual breakdown, but I think that my OCD was bound to emerge even if nothing particularly traumatising had occurred. I was a young woman who valued control, routine and certainty. Unfortunately, apart from the certainty that cishet men are often the worst, nothing much in life is predetermined. I, a person who as previously mentioned had a dual-coordinated wardrobe, was simply overwhelmed by the demands of adulthood. It was all flying at me like so much space debris, and I just didn't have the knowhow to get my deflector shield up in time.

Rather than seeking therapy, or, I don't know, learning to crochet, I got a tattoo. It was a simple, spidery-thin outline of a love heart. I say *was* because it no longer resembles its first incarnation. Once it healed, I noticed that the outline was very slightly uneven. This ... bothered me. I promptly returned to my tattoo artist and requested in a no-nonsense tone that he even it out. Well, when I say no-nonsense, I mean a tentative and apologetic tone, because I'm nothing if not a resolute people-pleaser. He obliged, thickening the line slightly to smooth out the wonky edge, but made a point to tell me that tattoos never turn out picture-perfect.

Once my tattoo had healed anew I examined it closely, rotating my wrist from side to side and stretching my skin to subtly contort the shape. I was certain it was still wonky, and so I went back. Some may say my behaviour was obsessive. Some may even use the word compulsive. Both would be rude, but correct. My artist acquiescently went at it again, but this time with a notably arched eyebrow. The fourth time, his eyebrow was accompanied by a tightly pursed mouth. By the fifth iteration, he was, if you'll pardon the subtle brow pun, absolutely browbeaten. At this point, the outline was so thick there was more ink visible than skin. I watched as black ink muddled with blood filled in the remaining empty space like rainwater in a swimming pool. Afterwards, I left the studio while he pointedly flipped the 'open' sign to 'closed'.

I spoke about all of this with my psychologist, Sharon. The all-encompassing perfectionism, the exaggerated fight-or-flight instinct, the fact that I'd never been taught to ride a bike, which, despite her telling me to let it go, felt like a crucial piece of information in my aetiology. I kept up with the CBT and the ABC and the inane discussion of all things *BtVS*. Eventually, and there's no way for this not to feel like either an oversimplified or jarring transition, I started to feel better. It was as though I'd been carrying a heavy backpack and gradually it started feeling lighter. First just barely, maybe by half a kilo. Eventually, it was like I had a twelve-litre backpack with only a wallet inside. I started my journey towards reasonable mental health by taking three weeks off work (acknowledging here that I am privileged enough to have been able to do so), and spent them mostly just doing my therapy homework and trying to stay on top of the basics of self-care like showering and drinking water. Showering was especially difficult for me in those days, and not in a Jake Gyllenhaal finding it unnecessary to bathe kinda way.[27] I felt keenly naked and vulnerable when, well, naked and vulnerable. Being nude left me open to intrusive thoughts about nudity, and the rest. Nonetheless in an act of radical exposure therapy, I forced myself to be exposed (to myself, not in an exhibitionist kinda way), over and over again: until eventually it got easier.

My journey to a place of relative stability was staggered with highs and lows, including one full-blown panic attack. It was precipitated by an extended bout of insomnia, my mind whirring with nonsensical and hellish thoughts. Luckily, Sharon had taught me a meditation exercise in which I was to envision a feather lightly drawing a line down my entire body from head to toe. At the same time, I had to practise slow, mindful breathing. However, rather than being relaxing or grounding, I started to have intrusive thoughts about feathers lightly tickling inappropriate people in inappropriate places. I couldn't stop the barrage of thoughts. Forget diaphragmatic breathing: I couldn't *breathe*. I felt lighthearted and dizzy, my arms were tingling, and I had a tightness in my chest like The Hulk was squeezing my heart. When it finally passed, I lay stock-still, shaken up but thankfully aware of what it was and not mistaking it for a heart attack. I knew there was to be no sleep for me that night. Switching on the bedside lamp, I quietly snuck out to the living room, turned on the TV, and with the volume down low, resumed watching my beloved *Buffy*.

By the end of my three-week leave, I had binged all of *Buffy*, including the DVD featurettes. Over the full duration of

27. Wanshel, Elyse, 'Jake Gyllenhaal: "More and More I Find Bathing to be Less Necessary"'. 6 August 2021, huffpost.com/entry/jake-gyllenhaal-bathing_n_610 d642ae4b0cc1278bbc862.

the series, Willow in particular undergoes a dramatic series of transformations. Starting off as a self-effacing piece of wallpaper, she meets the soft-spoken Wiccan Tara Maclay in college, and falls deeply in love. Willow practises witchcraft with studious dedication, but by series six is addicted to the black arts. She's out of control, unable or unwilling to stop herself from abusing magic. By the final season, she's clean and sober, in the magical sense. However, she's unwilling to use her powers for fear of falling into an addiction spiral again and hurting those around her. By the show's conclusion (spoiler alert, but c'mon, you've had since 2003 to get on board), she is forced to access her abilities in order to save the world: no pressure or anything. Willow performs a powerful spell that activates multiple Potential Slayers around the world. Her spell defies Buffy's inherited legacy of being the only active Slayer in the world, instead making her power a collective one. Willow says of the spell that it transcends anything she has ever attempted before, and further describes it as being an utter loss of control.[28]

Willow doesn't just go from being a pasty nerd to a murderous villain to an ethereal goddess overnight. It takes seven long seasons of devoted study and painful introspection. She often slips up, and people inevitably get hurt. But by the end, Willow transforms into a white witch, in a reversal of the black hair and blue veins lewk from season six, when she went on a vengeance rampage and nearly destroyed the world. Her character arc and final resolution are not evidence of Willow mastering total control: in fact, it's the opposite. She's able to emerge a victor because she works at it and, ultimately, because she cedes control over that which she cannot master.

Similarly, Buffy must let go of her identity as the ultimate I'm-not-like-other-girls girl, in order to share her immense power with girls around the world. She has to relinquish some of her hard-won and tightly held control. Further, Buffy cannot defeat

---

28. Season 7, episode 22, *BtVS*, 'Chosen', written and directed by Joss Whedon, 2003.

The First Evil or its Turok-Han (ubervamp) henchmen alone: she has to ask for and accept help. I had to put in years of hard work to get to a place where I could bear the burden of my brain backpack (okay, so maybe that metaphor has run its course). I had to refuse the impulse to enact compulsive behaviours, and in doing so I willingly invited risk and danger. I would interlace my fingers and count to ten, waiting for the compulsion to pass, not unlike a craving. Eventually, after doing this over and over again, I came to see it as a kind of proof that something bad could happen, but it might not. And if it did, I could probably deal with it.

Now over a decade since I had a nervous breakdown, I rarely perform compulsive actions. If I have an intrusive thought, I'm usually able to laugh it off (because, let's face it, sometimes they *are* very funny). I'm presently not on any medication, but I attach no stigma to it: if I need it, I need it. I practise yoga and meditation weekly if not daily, and I still regularly see a psychologist.

Recently, I was soaking up the late-winter sunshine by meditating in a nearby park. About five minutes into the session, I realised that I was low-key giving off paedophile vibes. Picture this: I was sitting upright on a wooden park bench, brim of my cap pulled down low, dark sunglasses, baggy clothes. Straight ahead, small children were swinging on the monkey bars. I considered removing my sunnies so it was obvious I wasn't staring unblinkingly at the underage people, but instead I chose to regather my focus and continue meditating. It was only afterwards that I realised how profound a shift the moment indicated. Rather than fixating on the implications of the quasi-offensive thought, I'd let it take shape in my brain, acknowledged it without judgement, and moved on. I let all the noise and distraction both inside and outside my mind just be, just … namastay. Anyway, obviously that's kind of meditation's whole deal, but for me to be able to just be with my thoughts … well, it was gratifying.

I cringe to write this, but I've also found exercise to be a potent form of self-care. I cringe because my entire identity when I was younger revolved around an anti-sports mentality, and also because the fitness and wellness industries can be irrefutably toxic. But I can't deny that when I'm working out, I'm present only in the movements: I'm in my body, not my brain. It releases endorphins, and it keeps my body fit(ish) and strong(ish). Sometimes I do strength training, sometimes cardio, sometimes yoga and sometimes dance: although dancing usually involves me spinning around to Earth, Wind & Fire in my living room while buzzed on beer, so it may not contribute to a calorie deficit.

Before I start sounding like I'm one green smoothie away from an enlightened state, I should clarify that none of these things equal immediate sanity or serenity. If someone confides in you that they have OCD, saying 'Why dontcha meditate?' or 'Have you tried eliminating refined sugars?' is not going to be helpful and may land you a well-deserved right hook to the jaw. For me, these are practices of self-care that incrementally and cumulatively contributed to a slow improvement in my mental health. None of them were magic bullets, and crucially, they're far easier to do when you're already in a Zen frame of mind. Basically, what I'm saying is, for me, first came the extra-strength pharmies and intensive therapy, then came the ashwagandha tea and ommmmm-ing. Only then could I namaslay the anxiety (sorry not sorry).

Also, despite being in a very manageable mental place, I still live with OCD: and I likely always will. In times of heightened stress, I might find myself subconsciously retracing my steps or rewashing my hair while ruminating and counting. Even in the most chillaxed of times, I still check I've locked the front door several times every time I leave work. Sometimes I even double back to pull on the handle once or twice more for good measure: honestly, I'm surprised the cops have never questioned me on suspicion of B&E.

Half the time, I don't even notice that my brain is spitting out intrusive thoughts or that I'm performing a counting ritual inside my head. It does mean I have to stay on top of things lest they spiral, but it also means that I'm okay with enduring the presence of residual OCD. It's sort of like there's a monkey clapping cymbals in my brain. It used to be excruciatingly loud, but now he's lined his cymbals with cotton wool, and he isn't playing twenty-four hours a day. More often than not he's sitting in a corner, happily eating a banana. He just plays occasionally when he's bored and there's nothing good on telly.

I may always live with a background hum of anxiety, and I do need to keep on top of all things cerebral. However, if I find myself really wigging out, I'm confident that I know what to do. I've also learned that sometimes my anxiety can work *for* me, alerting me to the presence of actual danger and keeping me safe. If I assess the situation and find there isn't an actual threat, I can just tell my monkey mind, *thanks but no thanks*. It may disagree with me, but eventually my racing heart will slow and my sweaty palms will dry. Most of the time, the threat isn't real or the risk isn't substantive. The reward, on the other hand, can be massive.

A few years ago, I moved from Brisbane to Sydney to do my PhD. I had returned to university a few years after dropping out in order to study creative writing. To my happy surprise, I loved it. It was the polar opposite of my first experience in tertiary education. The first time around, I went to uni because it seemed like the logical thing to do. I chose journalism simply because it involved reading and writing, and I didn't know what I wanted to do or be beyond maybe working with words. It wasn't a good fit, but more than this I just wasn't mentally prepared. The second time around, I was ready. I craved intellectual stimulation and a pathway to a more enriching career. Also, a customer had recently shat all over the floor at work: it was highly motivating.

This time, I made fast friends amongst my cohort of like-minded peers, and we had stirring and thought-provoking conversations at the café and uni bar about anything from books to boys. I made the dean's list for academic excellence, and I went on to complete my honours year, graduating with first-class honours and receiving the coveted university medal. The awards and accolades weren't the be-all and end-all, although I admit they did provide some delicious external validation.

Unlike in my fantasy, uni wasn't always a walk in the park, but this time I leaned into the uncertainty and difficulty. The first time I was like Xander in season one, admitting to hiding in the face of danger.[29] This time I was like Xander in … well, actually I actively aspire to *not* be like Xander in any season, now I think about it. The fragile masculinity is just … too much. Anyway, it was a no-brainer for me to do my PhD next. I chose Sydney because I was offered a scholarship, and beyond this I was ready for a change of scenery and I craved the challenge. My family didn't approve. Like the Weird Sisters in *Macbeth*, they foresaw toil and trouble. Unlike the Weird Sisters in *Macbeth*, they weren't into it. We fought about my decision, and relations between us were strained for a while, but my mind was made up. I acknowledged but didn't absorb their fears, while acknowledging but challenging my own.

Unfortunately for me, the PhD was not what I'd expected. I felt like more of an imposter than I ever had in my first stab at undergraduate study, and I wasn't prepared for the isolation and lack of structure. However, despite the unforeseen difficulties, I didn't regress into old, destructive patterns. I was able to recognise that I was okay and that I would continue to be okay. Sure, on multiple occasions I came home from meetings with my supervisors sobbing until my eyes were red, but that's just called *processing*. Recovering from or learning to live peaceably with OCD can take months or years. Learning to live with yourself, which is really what it's all about, can take a lifetime. Learning to love yourself might be the greatest gift of all, but that one's harder still. And I don't just mean to perform at karaoke, although it is famously atonal when delivered by anyone except Whitney and her

---

29. Season 3, episode 1, *BtVS*, 'The Witch', written by Dana Reston, directed by Stephen Cragg, 1997.

five-octave vocal range. So yeah, I was okay, as regards old OCD habits. However, I did experience a different kind of regression: that of disordered eating. I know, I know, I'm dropping more plot twists than an M. Night Shyamalan movie (I don't see dead people, but I've had many intrusive thoughts *about* dead people).

So how does disordered eating tie in to all this OCD business? Well, statistics suggest that women are generally at a higher risk of developing OCD than men (although men seem to experience an earlier onset and risk symptom worsening at a greater rate than women do).[30] As well, women are more likely to have comorbid conditions such as eating disorders.[31] Interestingly, the *Diagnostic and Statistical Manual of Mental Disorders* (DSM), lumps body dysmorphic disorder, hoarding, trichotillomania, excoriation and obsessive compulsive disorder together in the chapter 'Obsessive-Compulsive and Related Disorders.'[32] The high rate of comorbidity between eating disorders and OCD makes sense when you think about it. In anorexia and bulimia, thoughts about food and weight can be fittingly described as obsessional, and such thoughts often go hand in hand with ritualised eating behaviours. Furthermore, the act of purging after eating can temporarily (emphasis on *temporarily*) relieve anxiety, much like the short fix of OCD compulsions.

As well as OCD, I have a somewhat disordered history with food and my body. I'm careful to preface this admission with the caveat 'somewhat' because I don't classify myself as having had an eating disorder per se. However, I have experienced disordered thought

30. Emily Fawcett, et al., 'Women are at greater risk of OCD than men: A meta-analytic review of OCD prevalence worldwide'. *Pyschiatrist.com*, psychiatrist.com/jcp/ocd/ocd-prevalence-and-gender; Brittany Mathes, et al., 'Epidemiological and clinical gender differences in OCD'. *Current Psychiatry Reports*, 2019, 21(5), researchgate.net/publication/332597467_Epidemiological_ and_Clinical_Gender_Differences_in_OCD.
31. Ibid.
32. *Diagnostic and Statistical Manual of Mental Disorders*. American Psychiatric Association, 2014, psychiatry.org/psychiatrists/practice/dsm.

patterns around food and my body throughout my entire adult life, and I have a history of binge eating. When I say I binge eat, I don't just mean a doughnut here, a doughnut there. I'm talking about eating two large serves of dinner, a family bag of chips, several cupcakes and five or six slices of toast: and that's just the entree. During bad binges, I eat whatever's at hand, right up to and including dry food for my guinea pigs. I'm joking about that last one, but I really do eat and eat until I can no longer breathe or move with ease.

When I feel the need to binge, it's never because I'm hungry, and I can't just stop when I'm full. Afterwards I feel heavy, not just with food, but with the oppressive weight of self-loathing. Writer and producer on *Buffy the Vampire Slayer* Marti Noxon had her directorial debut with *To the Bone* in 2017, a movie about a young woman with severe anorexia nervosa. It was based largely on her own struggles with anorexia and starred Lily Collins in the lead role, who also has a history of anorexia. In an interview on the press junket for the film, Noxon explained that people think about anorexia as being control-based but, in her view, what is really driving it is a refusal or inability to engage deeply with one's emotions. She says that, for her, control is a convenient way to not have to feel uncomfortable or ugly feelings.[33] Of course, the irony is that exerting control is a reaction to the fear of losing control, and by depriving, purging or binging, control is inevitably lost. Your body controls *you*.

While I would argue that all eating disorders are fundamentally about the same thing, binge eating is the most obvious loss of control because shovelling piles of sloppy food into one's gob has immediate and obvious connotations of unrestraint. For me, binging correlates directly with OCD. In both instances, I would perform an action to control a thought or subdue a feeling, but by caving to the compulsion I would lose control over my own free will, not to mention my ability to sit in comfort.

---

33. '*To the Bone*: Why Marti Noxon used her directorial debut to tell such a personal story'. *Indie Wire*, 14 July 2017, indiewire.com/2017/07/to-the-bone-marti-noxon-interview-1201849254.

With the bingeing, the fear of losing control was multifaceted. Yes, I felt out of control around food, but the urge to eat really arose because I also felt out of control in other, unrelated areas of my life. Take my PhD. I was never a procrastinator, but during the three years it took me to complete my PhD, I watched more TV than in my entire life up until that point. With my undergrad and honours degrees, there had been at least a vague schedule, but in a PhD (especially one in the humanities which doesn't necessitate lab time) you devise your own timetable. Beyond this, though, I spent a long period of time having no clue what I was researching or how to research it. I was lucky to meet wonderful people through my degree, but initially I didn't even know my way around, let alone know many people. I felt alone and insecure.

My binge eating got worse than it ever had as I stress-ate my way through my doctorate. On top of the actual eating, I developed increasingly disordered thinking about my body. Where before my self-loathing had been mostly confined to the moments of a binge and the time directly following it, now I started hating the way my body looked more often than not. Despite being naturally thin, I suffered from dysmorphic thinking. I wouldn't restrict my intake of food very much, but I interpreted this as a lack of will power around food rather than indicative of something positive or healthy. I would think obsessively about food and, while I never counted calories or tried extreme diets, I occasionally verged on orthorexic thinking (a fixation on eating healthily and exercising), if not behaviours. My relatively newfound appreciation of exercise, which had initially granted me mental peace, now risked becoming one more thing to obsessively perform.

An article entitled 'Perfectionism in Women with Binge Eating Disorder' reports that perfectionism is a salient feature associated with women with anorexia and bulimia. It also states that perfectionism is observable in women who exhibit related symptoms of food disorders, such as restrictive dieting and a desire for thinness, but who do not quite align with the criteria for diagnosable eating disorders.[34] Hello, me. I am nothing if not a perfectionist, and in a PhD there are precious few milestones or moments in which you receive tangible proof of how well you are or are not doing.

Unable to make sense of my day-to-day life, or to predict what the future held, I shifted focus to my body as something I could, if not control, at least redirect my attention to. I would seek reassurance in a way that was eerily similar to that of OCD. Instead of asking, 'Are you sure I turned off my hair straightener?', I would talk about how bloated I felt, publicly berate myself for overeating or describe how much weight I'd gained, all in an attempt to receive confirmation that I was still slender. It wasn't always conscious, but sometimes it was. I know now how insensitive this behaviour was towards people who were in bigger bodies than mine or who may have had their own issues around food, but at the time I couldn't seem to help it. I would also perform checking behaviours: weighing myself and checking the mirror, squeezing the small amounts of flesh around my tummy and hips.

What was most upsetting was that *I knew better*. I knew about weight stigma and toxic diet culture. I was all *over* the systemic oppression and hyper-medicalisation of fat bodies. I follow @i_weigh and @drjoshuawolrich and @meganjaynecrabbe on Instagram, for crying out loud! I knew that I was thin and that even if I wasn't it wouldn't necessarily indicate *anything* unhealthy or unattractive. I knew, deep down in my hereditarily thin bones, that it was all meaningless and offensive and a waste of time, energy and the tiny sliver of happiness we have in this life. But, like the division between knowing and feeling within the OCD brain, I had a disconnect between what I distinguish as my 'feminist brain' and my 'feelings brain'. The guilt I felt over my fatphobia was almost worse than the guilt over the actual behaviour. And then,

---

34. Elizabeth M. Pratt, et al., 'Perfectionism in women with binge eating disorder'. *International Journal of Eating Disorders*, 2001, 29(2):177–86, researchgate.net/publication/11910757_Perfectionism_in_women_with_binge_eating_disorder.

like Bruce Willis finding out he was a ghost all along, another plot twist came my way. COVID-19 struck.

It's early days, but research suggests that overall, obsession and compulsion in people with pre-existing OCD has become more severe since the pandemic began. In particular, contamination symptoms got worse, and anxiety and agoraphobia in general seemed to become elevated. However, it's not all grim: those who have already undergone successful treatment, like myself, may actually have increased abilities and skills to deal with the uncertainty brought on by COVID-19.[35]

Like an Olympian training her whole life, or dare I say, a Slayer, people with OCD and other anxious conditions have spent years envisioning exactly this type of scenario. We catastrophise and prepare ourselves for the worst. Moreover, if we've managed to get a grip on our OCD, we've learned to accept the uncertainty, and face our fears. One blog post I read optimistically proposed that people with OCD may actually demonstrate how to live peaceably in times of extreme uncertainty even while feeling reasonable amounts of fear, and that the general public could look to the OCD community for their skills in managing anxiety.[36] Not to mention that we were carrying around hand sanitiser well before a global pandemic. Who's crazy now, huh? HUH?

In general, my mental health slightly worsened through the pandemic, along with everybody else's. As weeks turn into months, living with constant economic precarity, intermittent lockdowns and ever-present health concerns inevitably takes a toll. However, I was already well-versed in both excessive hand-washing and

---

35. Elizabeth Lawrence, 'How those with obsessive compulsive disorder cope with added angst of COVID'. *KHN*, 22 June, 2020, khn.org/news/how-those-with-obsessive-compulsive-disorder-cope-with-added-angst-of-covid.

36. Ethan S. Smith, et al., 'Why the OCD community holds the key to coping with COVID-19 anxiety'. *IOCDF*, 24 March, 2020, /iocdf.org/blog/2020/03/24/why-the-ocd-community-holds-the-key-to-coping-with-covid-19-anxiety.

coping with uncertainty. What's more, because of my three years doing my PhD, I was accustomed to working from home. I actually submitted my PhD in the middle of the first lockdown in Sydney, which I personally feel warrants extra credit. My OCD didn't begin manifesting in new and terrifying ways, and interestingly, my disordered food behaviours actually improved, if only slightly. I still experience moments of irrational self-loathing. I still fixate on food. I still feel guilty if I don't walk ten thousand steps in a day. However, all the time at home forced me to loosen my control a bit. I started cooking and baking with a renewed vigour, and while Gordon Ramsay would no doubt toss my rubbery sourdough loaves straight in the bin, I nonetheless relished in sampling the bread, fresh out of the oven and slathered with vegan butter. When my local gym closed down, I turned to less strenuous physical activity, instead enjoying Cher, Cindy Crawford and Jane Fonda aerobic workouts. I gained weight, and it made me uncomfortable, but I interrogated the validity of the discomfort, and did so in pants that fit comfortably. I did mindful eating activities when I felt the need to binge. It didn't always work. It still doesn't always work. At the time of writing, we are still in the midst of the pandemic, and I'm still in the midst of learning to love, or at least accept myself.

In season three, minor recurring character Lily says to Buffy that she is not good at taking care of herself. Buffy responds that it becomes easier with practice.[37] And if this piece has any moral message to it, it might just be that. With the right resources, and hopefully the right people supporting you, taking care of yourself gets easier. One day, over the phone, my mum told me she and my dad are proud of me. Not just because I was persevering with my doctorate, but also because of the strides I'd taken over the course of my time living here. I'd moved to a new city, travelled by myself overseas, put myself up for various professional opportunities and gone off my medication (and on again and off again, like Miley Cyrus and Liam Hemsworth).

---

37. Season 3, episode 1, 'Anne', *BtVS*, written and directed by Joss Whedon, 1998.

'When I think about where you were at twenty-one, and where you are now ...' Mum didn't finish her sentence, but I knew what she was leaving unsaid. Family in the Buffyverse is portrayed as disappointing: mothers are ineffectual, fathers are absent, and apparently Sunnydale has a one-child policy because nobody has a sibling. But in real life, my family were *my* Scooby Gang. The confusing and frustrating thing about family is that often their faults are also their strengths. My upbringing may have contributed to an acute stress response usually only seen in highly strung lab rats, but it also instilled in me the certainty that my family will always be willing to protect and guide me. As a woman in my thirties, I don't require an elaborate set of instructions for how to cross the road without getting hit by traffic. However, I'll take it if it means I can keep the memory of my parents driving me to the doctor's office and squeezing my hand, and of my brother calling me just to say he loves me.

When I was in the darkest days of my OCD, my family were there for me. My friends were too, once I let them in. You may remember me saying that one housemate in particular would just sit and listen to me, commiserating over my various woes. Once I was in better working order, that housemate and I started dating. He saw me at my most volatile and fragile mental state, and he *still* wanted to get to know me. We've since celebrated our twelve-year anniversary as a couple. He moved with me from Brisbane to Sydney, and we live together with two guinea pigs.

I didn't mention it before, because I don't want to inadvertently imply a male saviour narrative, or a saviour narrative, full stop. But the fact is I didn't do this alone. Maybe you or someone you know has OCD. Maybe you or they don't have as close a family as I'm lucky to have. Maybe you or they don't have many friends. And maybe you or they don't have a partner. That's okay. You can't just get over something like OCD without help, but that help can come from a trained professional, or even anonymous posters on Reddit describing their poop obsessions. Once you're a bit more centred within yourself, you will likely be in a place where you can foster more intimate connections. But it's even okay to only have the space for fictional friends, at first: those you find in books or on TV.

Clancy—my partner—and I are currently doing our annual Buffy re-watch. He's not as obsessed (pardon the word choice) as I am, but he enjoys it well enough. Lately, we watch more of it than we normally would, because we're both stuck at home in yet another lockdown. Watching it this time means more to me than it ever has. In a paper entitled 'Buffy, The Vampire Slayer as spectacular allegory: A diagnostic critique', Douglas Kellner argues that 'the allegory of BtVS does not produce a seamless whole or convey a unified system of messages, as did Christian allegory, but rather provides a more fragmented and contradictory postmodern set of meanings.'[38] It's impossible to find certainty in much of anything these days. I can't even guarantee that I can remain constant in myself. If my ebbing and flowing through the waters of OCD, binge eating and body dysmorphia has shown anything, it's that progress is incremental and fluctuating.

Likewise, the characters and plots of Buffy are hugely unstable: good characters like Willow or Angel turn evil, and evil characters like Spike turn good. What's more, the characters are volatile and their transformations are impermanent. Sometimes characters are even good and bad all at once. Giles sardonically tells Buffy that life is black and white, with good and evil being identifiable by their clothing, and the morally scrupulous heroes always coming out on top.[39] As viewers, we know that Giles' words are false. As Kellner writes, 'destructive events happen frequently in the series, characters and actions are fraught with ambiguity and contingency and the universe as a whole is highly insecure. Shit frequently happens in Buffy's world; death happens, relations

---

38. Douglas Kellner, 'Buffy, the Vampire Slayer as spectacular allegory: a diagnostic critique'. UCLA, pages.gseis.ucla.edu/faculty/kellner/essays/buffy.pdf.
39 Season 2, episode 7, 'Lie to Me', BtVS, written and directed by Joss Whedon, 1997.

break up and turn ugly, and happiness can rapidly dissolve.'[40] It's this—the truism that *shit happens*—that is both terrifying and comforting, and sometimes both at once. We, all of us, have the capacity to metamorphose into something new. Likewise, we all have the potentiality of backsliding. When I watch Buffy and her friends evolving and regressing, and even dying and coming back to life, I see myself.

Research on perfectionism, OCD and eating disorders suggests that women, and young women in particular, are especially susceptible to control-based issues. No doubt we can trace a great deal of it back to *cough* the patriarchy. The first mental disorder attributed to women, as early as Ancient Egyptian times, is hysteria, in which the cause of any manner of hysterical disorders was ascribed to the uterus moving around spontaneously within the body.[41] If you're unfamiliar with the medical community's history of diagnosing women with hysteria when they were really just horny and not allowed to vote, check out 'Women and hysteria in the history of mental health'. This paper breaks down the two dominant historical approaches towards women and mental disorders as being 'magic-demonological' and 'scientific'. The authors state that back in the day, women were seen as being susceptible to mental disorders, easily influenced by supernatural forces or 'organic degeneration', and guilty of sin and, well, spinsterhood.[42] I'm counting myself pretty lucky to live in the twenty-first century and to not get an involuntary exorcism when I go in for my regular pap smear.

As women, we are taught to inhibit ourselves, to contain ourselves, even to shrink ourselves: whether in body, mind or

---

40. Douglas Kellner, op. cit.

41. Cecilia Tasca, et al., 'Women and hysteria in the history of mental health'. *Clinical Practice and Epidemiology in Mental Health*, 2012, 8: 110–119, clinical-practice-and-epidemiology-in-mental-health.com/contents/volumes/V8/CPEMH-8-110/CPEMH-8-110.pdf.

42. Ibid.

desire. We are taught to fear being seen as too much. I am, on occasion, a lot. I may even be out of control. The world is, always, out of my control. Ergo, this makes me occasionally feel … well, hysterical. I used to be unable to accept anything less than one hundred per cent perfection and total control. But now, at the wizened age of thirty-three, I'm learning to embrace the magic-demonological by letting the demons in.

During an especially stressful day recently, I took five to perform the meditation exercise my shrink Sharon had encouraged me to do all those years ago. I went into my bedroom, lay down on the bed and shut my eyes. I envisioned myself lying in a canoe as it drifted slowly downstream. My mind was restless with thoughts, and one in particular was making its presence known to me. I inhaled and exhaled deeply. Lifting my head out of the canoe, I saw a shadow on the rocks, and forced myself to squint until it came into focus. There was no mistaking it: my OCDemon. It looked remarkably like The Master, ancient vampire and Buffy's original nemesis from season one. It snarled at me, dove headfirst into the water and swam quickly until it reached the boat. Fighting against the fear, I willed it to approach. It reached out a hand, as though to wrest me from the boat and pull me into the muddy water. Ten years ago I would have rowed briskly away. This time, I leaned over and reached out my own hand, helping it into the boat. Whaddya know? It wasn't so scary up close.

When I was about two-thirds of the way to relative recovery, I got another tattoo. It was my biggest one yet, based on a piece of fan art I found on Tumblr. It features a cartoonish portrait of Buffy with the words 'Buffy Summers, Our Lady of Protection'. It took hours and cost more money than I'm comfortable ever admitting to my mother. It's not perfect. The mouth is a bit weird, and the lettering is slightly crooked. I got it touched up when some of the colour dropped out, but for the most part I left the imperfections as they were. After all, as the years go by, it's bound to fade and blur, as my skin sags and wrinkles. My body will change, maybe getting smaller, likely getting bigger. Nothing is static. But with my patron saint of protection looking over me (or more accurately, up at me from her vantage point on my left upper thigh), I feel okay.

In 'Becoming, Part One', the love of Buffy's life, tormented vampire Angel, has lost his soul and is hell-bent on sending the world, well, to hell. Whistler (half-demon responsible for bringing Buffy and Angel together in the first place) espouses his view that Angel's turn to darkness is not the be-all and end-all: unless, you know, he manages to end it all. It's not what happens to us that counts, Whistler declares. No, what really matters is how we react afterwards. It's in those moments that a person discovers who they really are.[43] In the climactic battle scene between the two former lovers, unfolding in the season two finale, 'Becoming, Part Two', Angelus taunts Buffy. He asks her what is left once she's stripped of her friends, weaponry, and even hope. He goes to fell her with her own sword, and it seems all is lost. Until Buffy grips the blade between her bare hands, looks up at him, and with icy resolve answers that what is left when all else is gone, is herself.[44]

As I look down at my Buffy portrait, I find a resolve in myself I didn't always know was there. Nowadays, I feel like I don't need Buffy to protect me. I'm perfectly capable of taking care of myself. But even so, I like to know she's there as I gradually become who I'm meant to be. Becoming, part one, and two, ad infinitum.

---

43. Season 2, episode 7, 'Becoming, Part One', *BtVS*, written and directed by Joss Whedon, 1998.
44. Season 2, episode 8, 'Becoming, Part Two', *BtVS*, written and directed by Joss Whedon, 1998.

# Love and Other Obsessions

Martin Ingle

*Because of Jordan*

## Lorraine

My first love came on the same day as my first anxiety attack. It was wonderful but terrifying, and in fact so much of both at the same time that I spent the entire day literally trying not to throw up.

Okay, so it was either love or the quiche I ate for lunch. But when you're hunched over a toilet bowl poised ready to vomit and/or shit at any moment, then really what's the difference?

After film school, a group of us had unbelievably been given the opportunity to go to the Cannes Film Festival—basically the biggest international film event of the year, glitzy and prestigious on the south coast of France and the kind of place where a dozen or so bright-eyed kids from Brisbane had no business being at all. We could only afford to stay in a shitty backpackers hostel in Nice, a whole separate town and forty-minute train ride away from the actual festival. (The rumour was our travel agent had misheard 'Cannes' as 'Cairns' and booked us the wrong trip, in the most Australian move ever. The actual Cannes is a tiny town and literally all the accommodation books out almost a year in advance.) Still, we didn't much care that we were bunking with the bed bugs a whole city away. It felt like we were at the peak, looking down on our lives yet to unroll.

And sure enough, Cannes was the furthest thing from the quiet, inoffensive Brisbane suburbs we could imagine. If we'd only ever heard the echoes of show business, here was the actual din. We slept in grotty bunk beds one night and walked the red carpet feet away from Chris Rock the next; we watched in awe as a manic/coked-up Cuba Gooding Jr screamed '*Viva la France!*' into the mic at a sunset beachside premiere of his latest war epic; my best friend Jazz and I stumbled across Michael Haneke on the street just days before he won the Palme d'Or; in a particularly treasured memory, one bright, cool evening a café owner cheerfully dished out free champagne to us in the cobblestone street as we listened to an acoustic French trio play 'Seven Nation Army' by The White Stripes. In a classic Aussie tradition, one of us even had a cheeky vom in a cute French laneway on the walk back to the train one night, too. When you're twenty-one, it's easy to get drunk on things. On all these things.

To believe you can earn a living from making movies is delusional enough, so Cannes attracts us dreamers naturally, and then hooks us forever. For two weeks they create the place of your dreams, and it works. You believe anything is possible, because here it is in front of you. All these other dreams are coming true in front of my eyes—so why not The Big One™?

Like most of us at that age, for years I'd dreamed of meeting that Somebody who would fulfil me, complete me, understand me, quench my loneliness and blah blah blah. I mean that literally, by the way; I'd had actual dreams imagining this very specific person who I hadn't even met yet: *my other half; my soul mate; my destiny; The One* … you've seen the brochure. It felt like the Universe was giving me signs, telling me to keep an eye out for when She would appear. I was a believer, even if I didn't admit it. I'd only recently lost God, too—a huge, fundamental life change for the grandson of a priest, let me tell you. Even though I didn't technically have those beliefs anymore, I still carried their ghosts.

I had always been too chickenshit to properly ask anybody out, so it was amazing enough on that one night in Cannes when Jazz convinced me to turn around and run back to the beachside party I'd just left to ask for the number of the American girl working the door. Even more surprising was when she gave it to me. Quite the sudden romantic rush, I tell ya, dressed in a suit, sprinting through the streets of a quaint French town at midnight with your best friend so you don't miss the last train home and get stranded. You could hear the soundtrack.

I'm not sure why it's embarrassing for us to admit we're romantic. Vulnerability isn't cool, I suppose. Cynicism is more mature. Today I manage to wriggle around the awkwardness and shame of this story by saying I was young. I'd just turned twenty-two in the French sun. Newly graduated, arm in arm with friends looking out into the Mediterranean, we were at the precipice of something. You could feel it. Truthfully, I had no idea what expanse lay in front of me. Maybe it was just chance that pushed me slightly the wrong way. Maybe there was no other way I could have fallen. Maybe I was just a fart waiting for a struck match.

She looked strangely like that girl from my dreams, too. Dark hair, pale skin, and not to mention an accent—which only made her more dreamy. See, Americans really only existed in movies. They occupied that structured, optimistic, glamorous, dream-like world I'd grown up immersed in and fantasising about. And here was one in front of me, confident and intelligent and a total film nerd to boot. It's so silly. I can't even say it was her specifically who tripped the switch. Each year, each movie, each pop song and each sermon and each unguarded daydream had stacked me higher and higher like Jenga. I was primed and just ready enough.

We met up at a café at 10am and about five minutes later it was midday and I had three empty pots of tea in front of me. I was floored by her. But the trouble only really came later when, alone, I grabbed a quiche from the local bakery and started to stroll around the sunlit streets, oily paper bag in hand, pastry flakes on my collar and an odd flutter in my chest. That's when it hit.

I suddenly became aware of my rushing, insecure heartbeat. I quickened through the Cannes laneways. It was hot outside, wasn't it, and cold too. The more I started to think about it, the more I started to realise this was it—*Holy shit!; this is The Moment; this was The Person*—and the quicker I had to walk. I had to sit down. I had to stand up. I had to slow down. I had to throw up. I had to shit. *Did I? Didn't I?* Imagine the most scared, the most nauseous and the most excited you've ever been: combine it, double it, and swallow it, and you can understand why after a few hours of this

I found myself on my knees in front of Jazz, buzzed out of my mind and keeled over in fear and confusion.

I decided to retreat to the Screen Australia office—a community space in a fancy Cannes apartment for Australians to congregate, network, set up meetings and generally feel important. A hub of filmmakers, producers, distributors, students, journalists and critics, and here was skinny little me, locked in the marble bathroom, hunched over the loo in panic. *Please oh please don't let me shit my pants in front of Margaret and David.* That's two and a half stars from me.

Love and mental illness have always been inseparable for me. It's hard to tell the difference sometimes. Still, despite my brain's best efforts, over the years I've somehow managed to stumble my way through a few vastly different romantic partners since that day with the quiche and the American, but they've all been haunted by this same very unromantic spectre of mental illness: the panic-inducing attempt at first sex; the hippie who tried to loosen my vice-like mind with magic mushrooms; even when I fell in love with another person with OCD. None of this was easy; in fact each new quivering attempt at intimacy was an active choice to swim against the tide of my obsessional fears. My brain was screaming at me not to, but for some reason I persisted.

Throughout it all, there was always both a hope and a danger of some vague future version of myself that I was constantly creating, whether I liked it or not. At every moment, I stood at a fork in the road towards two very different futures. I could either side with my illness and do what it wanted me to do—safer, but sicker—or I could step the other way, through my worst fears but towards that healthier version of myself on the horizon that I had no guarantee even existed. The choice was never easy. Most of the time I lost. But on the darkest nights, exhausted and bleeding and crying and smacking myself over the head to try to make it stop, there was always some deep pilot light that kept me going: knowing that the forks I'd taken had literally led me here, and I didn't want to be here anymore.

My picture of these years is hazy. When I plunge my face into the murky swirl of these memories, certain shapes stand out and others timidly take form, but on the whole they're fuzzy. Maybe, if what we know about memory is true, they're in a constant process of dissolving and remaking themselves, which is scary enough itself.

Some drift into my mind out of nowhere every now and again, floating back to me on a circular current every few years— *Hey, remember this shit? What the fuck was that about?*—before disappearing again.

A few are tangible signposts driven in deep and secure, marking significant events. I'm not sure when my brain decided that these were the memories to remember.

And a few—a rare few—I deliberately try to forget because I desperately don't want them to become one of these signposts. If I can't control my thoughts, at least I can control how I remember them, right? I can control my story. These ones are often so traumatic I'm actually successful at it. Trauma makes you forget; in this way it's on your side.

If my thoughts are all recorded by a court stenographer for one final apocalyptic day when I'm forced to answer for all of them, I want each one to be explainable. I've lived with this for so long now, I've had so many horrific intrusive thoughts, that it's literally impossible to remember them all. I've learned this only over time: the icy avalanche piles up to the point you become numb. There's simply too much horror to hold in your head at once. So you start to forget. This is trauma too.

Still, how can this be? How can such an important chapter have so many blank pages? Writing about it here is an attempt to fill them in, I suppose. But I don't know how many of these words to truly trust.

I wonder, reading this, how the Loves in my life will react when they hear my recollection of events? How differently do they remember the conversations we had differently? In the narrative of their own heads, where do I sit? Do they even remember these things at all? Have I conveniently forgotten the stuff that might make me look bad? And how much of what I *do* confidently recall will even survive through the filter of ego and try-hard flowery language and attempts at good storytelling to finally arrive safe and true on these pages? Impossible to say.

The alternative, though, is to be so paralysed by doubt that I never say anything at all and so never risk saying something misremembered or even remotely misleading. This would be easy to do; just curl up, shut up, never tell this story—or if I do, saturate it with so many caveats and *on-the-other-hands* that I'm thoroughly protected from doubt while at the same time being absolutely fucking insufferable. I suppose that's what I'm doing right now. Part of the process of getting better is learning what things to hold on to lightly and what things are okay to confidently throw my weight behind, even if I feel doubt. Much of the time I just don't know which to choose—and recovery means accepting that too.

For better or worse, I've decided to write this love story down, like this, in this order. The fuzzy memories forced into solid black-and-white. It is a love story. Will you be able to predict which one of these Loves I eventually end up with? As you meet them you can guess along the way; be my guest! Tweet it at me, you might save me a lot of grief.

I'm still not sure if that day in Cannes was actually love or just a bad quiche, by the way. I never saw the American again, of course. We met up for dinner that night (I hardly ate), hugged awkwardly and then parted ways forever. She wasn't interested, I guess. Yeah, I know, I know: in the context of everything, a little one-day crush on a girl I hardly knew is pathetic, embarrassing to even mention. But I tell you, for that idealistic, immature, romantic boy, the experience was like an anchor dropped off a speeding boat. And for a while I was just about sunk. I spent the next year or so riding a wave of rising and falling panic attacks, spontaneous nausea and wildly irrational fears. Any kind of intimacy with somebody was now a Pavlov's Dog cue to—literally—panic. I couldn't even glance at a person I was attracted to on the bus without feeling my stomach creeping up my throat again. Not to mention I couldn't bear to eat quiche for a while.

This continued all the way up until my first sexual encounter about a year later. Her eerily recognisable dark hair and pale skin didn't help soften the trigger, regardless of how sympathetic and wonderful she was with this shivering lapsed Christian virgin in front of her.

It's an odd feeling of performance almost, like your body is on display and constantly being watched. I had hardly eaten the past couple of days; I was already skinny enough, and must've been basically skeletal by that point. This wasn't simple virginity nerves—embarrassing *American Pie*-type inexperience that would make a funny story one day. No, this was something more. I had the ominous sense there was some un-uncrossable line that I was about to step over, and that I would never be the same again once I had. I was twenty-three and I had never been naked with somebody in the same room. This was new. This was dangerous.

I have something called a pectus excavatum, which is where my sternum, rather than grow straight across bridging my ribs, caves in on itself just a little bit. It's very mild and doesn't cause any troubles other than aesthetic. Kinda looks like whoever my sculptor was gave me a swift jab to the chest while I was still setting. It wasn't like this when I was a teenager. Over years of growth spurts and severe asthma episodes my ribcage would pop and crack like a knuckle, I guess slowly caving in my breastbone.

I could also easily feel things back then. A dramatic little shit, *I burned, I pined, I perished*; every crush could be my soulmate incarnate. I was the lead character in a romantic story destined for dramatic twists and turns and a happy ending promised me by the movies I devoured. I ached for these scenes and looked out for them everywhere because there was no doubt. I was bursting. Now, with my smothering anxiety and concave chest, I wonder if I just don't have room in there for a raw and swollen heart.

Looking back, all of the anxiety, pain and confusion that followed The French Quiche Incident, foreign and sudden and terrifying though it was, was only a rudimentary warm-up to the truly obsessional thoughts that would soon take over my brain. I didn't know it then, but this was only a taste; a dip of the toe; the Devil's herald warning of the coming of the beast. I had only unlocked the door my brain was about to fling open.

There's a theory that the brain chemistry of somebody in love matches that of somebody with obsessive compulsive disorder. I remember reading about that study some time before I got OCD, before I even knew what this thing called OCD really was, but now—if true—I totally see the similarity. It's single-minded. It's impossible to switch off. It's irrational; you could even say delusional. You're not motivated by logic but by feeling. You're not concerned with the mechanics but more with *the unstoppable, burning rocket fuel.* Why tinker with the engine when the *goddamn machine is on fire?!*

Most importantly, this kind of love and this kind of obsession are both ultimately negative. Sorry, but it's true. It's literally disordered. And, despite the temptation, it's not to be deified or romanticised either. Your obsession becomes unhealthy, and yeah, your own 'love' harms you—and the very people you claim to love.

Looking back on it all, I have to ask myself: when so many of my loves have been ruined by my obsessions, which do I truly love more?

## 2015, my bathroom

It's only been two years since the thoughts started, but my God, it feels like two decades. Two years and a couple of months actually—I can pin it down to one specific winter just after I turned twenty-three that I witnessed my thoughts slowly, exponentially and unstoppably snowball out of my control. Every single moment of every single day since then has been saturated, drenched, washed-out, in one repulsive, putrid colour of sheer fucking doom.

*So dramatic, Martin.* Yeah, I know. But how else can you describe these thoughts to someone? It's doom—it really is.

Dear God. I was so full before this, wasn't I? I mean I was still an insecure, shy, idealistic kid, but come on, I was open at least! I was curious! I was creative! I laughed. I dreamed. Life stretched out in a boundless plain in front of me, and I was eager to explore, to grow—to love. I threw myself at dreams and marvelled at the beautiful people I could meet and the beautiful ways I could be challenged. New ideas were things to embrace, seek out and absorb. New emotions were a wondrous and confusing part of the package. I was young, thirsty and keen to fill my cup. I liked myself. I knew I was a good person. Until this.

Now here I find myself, two years later, on my hands and knees in the mouldy bathroom of our dingy sharehouse, trying to figure out how best to scrub my piss out of the toilet floor.

This house is old, practically a wooden shack with a lick of mustard paint. In the kitchen you can look straight down and see the dirt ground through clumsy gaps in the floorboards. But hey, it's what we can afford. Up high on stilts, it literally sways in the wind; we sit on the back deck and watch the bougainvillea vines comically jump and rock as our third housemate has vigorous sex at the complete opposite end of the house. This is what your twenties should be about, right? Parties, poverty and sexual awakening! I, on the other hand, am falling. I won't masturbate again for six years. Right now I can't even touch my penis to go to the toilet.

I'll never forget the smell of this bathroom—I spend a lot of time here. Sopping wet timber, eucalyptus, various brands of hand sanitiser and cleaning products. And humid, always humid—everything gets sealed in when you're having four-hour showers and refuse to open a window. I'm smothered by both thoughts and steam. Mould and gunk spread across the ceiling. Paint peels and curls on every surface. It's particularly tricky because I won't dry myself with a towel these days either so I have to figure out how to air-dry, essentially in a fucking rainforest. I've developed a technique of sort of squat-thrusting on the spot to push air around my bits like a makeshift bellows. Genius. Everything that dangles clumsily slaps back and forward and it sure takes a while, but hey it's better than the horror of the alternative.

I've been practically counting the days since the winter of 2013, acutely aware of the pain of every passing moment, and yet totally detached, living in another world inside my head, witnessing my life roll by in front of my eyes. It's been like this, all day, every day, and yet it somehow *still* seems like a temporary crisis, a brief period that I'll get over soon and things will go back to normal. It truly does feel like decades ago at the same time as it feels like only yesterday. The old me seems so frustratingly still within reach. Every day I'm straining for his hand. If I can just solve this. If I can just figure this out. If I can just *Jesus Christ get my piss off of the goddamn floor!*

When you're terrified of going to the toilet, you put it off for as long as possible. I've started to wet myself sometimes simply because I've held it for too long. If I don't fully piss my pants then it's a frantic last-second attempt to get to the toilet, drop trou without touching my genitals and try to aim, which anyone with a penis will tell you is practically Olympic. In this whole process, a few drops can sneak their way out—which, because you can feel the banks inevitably breaking as you dashwaddle across the room, follows you in a trail of piss breadcrumbs along the floor.

Fuck. Fuckitty fuck. I've got to get it off the floor. What kind of person would let that go? How can I? My housemates are going to walk here. Coupla sheets of loo paper aren't going to cut it either. Imagine what's left behind … *imagine what you can't see … imagine who else will have your piss on them by tomorrow … you may as well be wiping it on them yourself, and willingly … gleefully … maybe pleasurably—NO!*

So now here I am, still—who knows how much time has passed—scrubbing the grout between these tacky 1980s choc-brown tiles, trying to save myself from my thoughts, and the world from myself. How oh how did it come to this? This is a far cry from that optimistic, wide-eyed young guy sprinting through the streets of Cannes at midnight.

Freeze and preserve me on a day, one blissful glorious mindless day just twenty-four hours, a minute, one second before all this started, and that guy, even with all his anxiety and nausea and petty emotional drama would have no idea the cliff edge he was approaching. Take me back there. Dear God, take me back.

## Helene

I can clearly separate my life into two distinct chunks: the Martin before and the Martin after the winter of 2013. Chalk and cheese. People must feel that way about other significant life events: graduating, moving cities, getting married, losing a loved one … any of these gear-shifts that suddenly change the course of your life and make it easier to visualise chapters. I've had those sorts of things too, but what happened to me that winter was something else entirely, something truly catastrophic, and it all happened inside my own head. Within the space of a few weeks I was practically unrecognisable to myself. It was like I'd been suddenly transplanted into a completely new brain. And it was something I could never tell a soul.

It started very simply. Just a question: what if I'm not what I seem? What if I'm not what I think I am? What if I'm somehow, secretly, irreparably broken? What if this is a truth so buried, so dysfunctional, so unimaginably horrific, that I've hidden it, even from myself, as a defence mechanism? What if there's been evidence of this secret throughout my entire life and I've just ignored the signs until now? What if I'm dangerous? What if I'm bad? What if I'm evil and perverted in the most extreme way imaginable? A cannibal? A rapist? A paedophile? What if I get private pleasure out of imagining human flesh when I'm eating lunch; or from a dog licking my fingers; or from glancing at my sister in a bikini or …

… you get the idea. Some things are too awful to even say, even in a book explicitly about it, even around sympathetic ears. Some things I've only ever said to my psychologist. And even working up that courage took me years.

The sad thing is that the original onset of these unwanted obsessional thoughts was one of the major motivations for me to ask out my first serious girlfriend, Helene, who I ended up seeing for around six months. It had only been a few weeks of these obsessions: at that early point I was just so overwhelmed and confused by the sudden darkness and persistence of the intrusive thoughts that I needed to do something—*anything!*—to convince myself that I was somehow still normal. I didn't understand what was going on and I needed an answer as soon as I could. Diving right into a relationship (which was something I had been terrified of since the Cannes thing) seemed like a defiant and active resistance to what I thought at the time was just a very intense and convincing manifestation of *l'olde français* anxiety. What I didn't realise is this was just the beginning of a completely new kind of disorder.

Want to know the difference between general anxiety and obsession? For me it honestly felt like a pretty natural progression moving from one to the other, albeit a thousand times worse. Moving from anxiety to obsession was like suddenly jumping up a few belts in karate but also losing my arms. It was similar but different and also much much worse.

OCD used to be classified as an anxiety disorder in the DSM— the manual doctors use to diagnose exactly what type of crazy you are—but in 2013 the American Psychiatric Association gave *Obsessive Compulsive and Related Disorders* its own shiny new special category (*lucky us!*) when they realised 'anxiety' didn't quite cover it. Weirdly enough, it was at this exact same time, in a banal Australian suburb across the other side of the world, that I developed my own OCD, without having any idea that's what it was. I got it at the exact same time the world was starting to 'get' it. Make no mistake, that makes me one of the lucky ones.

It's normal for people to live for *years*, sometimes *decades*, without knowing they have OCD—or even knowing what OCD actually is. I'm lucky I only had to live in that black hole for less than a year. That black hole is precisely where I was after these unwanted thoughts first entered my mind in 2013, when they lit such a painful fire under my arse that I had to take action to try to prove them wrong—by asking out Helene.

Helene was quite different to girls I'd been interested in in the past. Having lost my faith in God, and so losing a belief in a soulmate too, I was no longer looking for that girl from my dreams, The One. I didn't need somebody perfect. In the past I might have been momentarily interested in somebody only to dismiss her very quickly when I discovered some little thing that didn't fit in with my dream's or God's or Hollywood's ideal for who my capital-L Love should be.

Helene wore her flaws in public like beauty spots. She swore. She danced. She was a proud nerd. She wouldn't feel weird having her arm around me in front of my parents. Mum definitely disliked her, which probably only made me like her more. She was sarcastic and vibrant and had incredibly dark humour. And she would burp. Loud. In front of my friends. And I'm not sure she once apologised. I'm not sorry either, for any of it.

But as great as she was, my obsessive thoughts had their hooks in me more than she did. I remember those initial months as always on extreme high alert. I was simply overwhelmed and minddrunk, my brain constantly agape in a silent and invisible scream of terror, frustration and anger at this clusterfuck of confusion. I was drowning in my own thoughts. Looking back on it, I'm surprised I was able to function in a relationship at all. My mind was such a mess, and I was hiding it all from everybody, even Helene. It seemed like I was at the same time a pretender concealing his 'true' self from the world while also an honest man trying desperately to hold on to a hopeful past version of himself. I fluctuated from being disgusted with myself to being defiant and resistant in the face of fundamental doubts. Back then, every day was a terrifying battle with myself over my own mind. And nobody knew.

It does make me sad that what turned into the first real

relationship of my life had been tainted in my mind from the beginning because it was motivated by these fears. Helene was wonderful, but I was never going to remember a time when I was just simply and purely happy with her, as for me our relationship started because of these obsessional fears: because my confusion and distress motivated me to action where nothing else till then really could. *I'm not a pervert, damn it, I swear I'm not—and this is how I'll prove it!* Ain't that awful: that something so great can begin because of something so horrible. What it meant was that for me the relationship was somehow contaminated now (*watch that wording*), the beautiful photographic memories smeared with a frame of literal shit. Not remotely her fault of course, and not even mine. Just another thing to blame on this fucking illness.

There's a brilliant moment in a UK documentary special called *OCD Ward* where one of the subjects, an inpatient at a hospital, is encouraged to carry around a jar of urine (or maybe even just urine-coloured liquid) as an exposure therapy. He and his therapist decide to draw a face on it and give it a name. He makes a joke that one day he could name his kid the same as this jar of piss and how funny and insulting that would be. His doctor then rebuts that he certainly could name his kid after the jar of piss, but not as an insult—as a symbol of his great victory over OCD. Yes, he carried around a jar of piss with a face drawn on it, but this ridiculous thing turned out to not be disgusting at all; in fact it was his key out of his prison. It was a great thing, not a horrible thing.

Now, I never had to carry around a jar of piss. But I try to do this same sort of reframing. I can choose to look back on that first relationship with Helene as a great victory; a great defiance; a huge and brave step forward that a young clueless guy took in the face of an internal torture he couldn't understand. A bit dramatic maybe, but hey, it works. Rather than constantly pushing up against your thoughts, you can take a step back and let them fall.

Back when I was with Helene, I was learning how to be in a relationship at the same time as I was trying to figure out what was going on in my mind. Both were such huge and instant changes in my life that on the inside I felt like I'd been dismantled and badly reassembled almost overnight. My personality felt like a shallow performance, a memory of how I once was that I was recreating for the world's benefit. I was an egg scrambled in its own shell.

And I tried to get out of it. To fix it. I just wanted to enjoy my time with her and move on from these thoughts. I was trying desperately to remember what I was like only a couple of months before and to get back to that place. But no matter how I tried, it never worked. My brain was working different. I was different. It actually took me a long time to accept that, even long after my relationship with Helene ended about six months later. There really was no returning to that past Martin, even though I wanted to. I had missed out on the opportunity to live as other people live. I would never know what it was like to be in a relationship with only two of you. These thoughts were always there with me now, an invisible guardian demon.

I'm still friends with Helene. She lives in LA—ashamedly she wasn't the first or the last actress I would fall for (I guess despite constantly being proven wrong, my heart still does romanticise the movies). I never told her what was going on in my head during our time together, though. She knew a bit about my past anxiety troubles, sure, but nothing about this new kind of obsessional thinking. I deliberately chose not to tell her, in retrospect a good decision since I didn't understand it anyway. I'd never heard of intrusive thoughts back then. How could I explain them to somebody else?

The closest I got was on one of the last nights we were together. We knew we were going to end it in advance; she was moving to Sydney and we didn't want to do long distance. I thanked her for being there for me, even if she didn't directly help, even though she had no idea what was going on. I wanted to thank her for just being there. We held each other naked for the last time and cried happy tears.

## 2015 again, the bathroom floor

See? The beginning wasn't like this. I never gave a shit about contamination back then. My obsessions had nothing to do with actual physical stuff that I could see, feel, touch or clean. Those thoughts never even occurred to me. You wouldn't have caught me scrubbing the floor for hours like this. I marvel at those memories now; at the things I used to do without a second thought that now I would find impossible: something as simple as holding hands, or even eating—*my God, eating!* These days a meal is a few gulps of milk straight from the carton, or maybe a banana if I'm really careful not to touch the inside as I peel it. My pants are starting to fall off me. My psychiatrist says if this continues we will have to consider admission somewhere. He warns me: 'You don't want that.'

Even though it looks quite different, this is the same illness, apparently, as I had those first dark months of 2013 when I was with Helene. I've learned enough about OCD since then: the huge variety of forms it can take, the way it doesn't discriminate in age, gender or ethnicity across the entire world. I know I am just one of two to five per cent of the population with it. I've learned how the illness functions and how therapy works. I see a psychologist and psychiatrist and I've just started medication. I'm just as sick now as I was at the beginning, it's just that back then it was all happening *inside my head*. Now it's in the real world. Now it has physical form. Now I can scrub it from the bathroom floor as well as I can purge it from my mind (that is to say: not well at all).

It's been strange these past couple of years to know I have OCD but to still not do any traditional 'OCD' things. No wonder it takes people ages to even know they have it. I knew the danger of it devolving to a different form even back then. I distinctly remember one night not too long ago touching the garbage bin and deliberately *not* washing my hands as a way to test myself— to pre-expose myself to the idea of contamination I didn't feel existed. Yet.

Of course, I couldn't have predicted that the type of contamination that obsesses me now has nothing to do with bacteria or germs or illness or health, like around garbage. Actually the contamination I see all around me now is an extension of those original, fundamental fears about *who I am*. I'm scrubbing this floor, not because I'm afraid the coupla drops of piss will get someone sick, not because it's vaguely icky and gross, but because *it would make me a bad person if I didn't.*

*Because it's not just piss on this floor, is it, Martin?* No. No, there's something more here too. Something worse …

I've abandoned absolutely all sexuality since it's gotten this bad. It's been weeks—maybe months, I don't remember—but to be honest it's been slowly digging its fingernails in deeper and deeper since the beginning. I distinctly remember the morning I slapped a partner's hand away from me several times in bed because I couldn't erase a horrific sexual image from my head. That should've been a hint of where it was going. But it's gotten worse since I've started to see physical contamination too. Now I can't even *pretend* to be normal on the outside like with Helene. No, these compulsions started deep down inside and then sprouted out and out over years and years until now they are unhidable.

I already stopped trying to masturbate months ago, not that I'd be able to now anyway. Not in this new world. How on Earth can I be alone with my own thoughts in pleasure when they are so disturbingly out of my control even in *neutral* situations like cleaning this goddamn floor?! No. To have an intrusive sexual thought during active sexual pleasure would be unforgivable. It would feel even worse if I was alone: more perverted, more clandestine, more secretive somehow. No. It's better to throw up my hands and walk away from it all completely. Yes. As long as these thoughts exist, I will be celibate as a monk: it's the only moral choice. Amazing, isn't it? The religion of OCD has made me more of a puritan than when I was actually religious.

But neutering myself, even for this short time, has snowballed. See, when you don't ejaculate for a while, fluids other than piss start to leak out too. When my bladder is bursting and I'm squeezing every muscle down there … when I feel poop massage past my dormant and enlarged prostate … in the constant fluctuating rushing pressure of erogenous zones that haven't been activated for weeks … in other words: I'm backed-up and horny and my body is bloody confused. Who knows what the fluid is that leaks out? *Pre-cum? Lube? Semen? Prostate … juice?* Gross. Whatever it is, it's obviously sexual right? It wasn't there when I was ejaculating regularly. But here it is now, uncontrollably oozing from under my foreskin, dabbed and dried on the inside of my undies and undeniably trapped in my urethra.

The bathroom floor doesn't just have a few splashes of sterile urine, Martin; no, it carried with it these horrid fluids too, and with them all your predatory sexual potential. I may as well have just cum all over the goddamn floor. What kind of a sicko could let that go? Not me. That's not me. It's not me. I could never forgive myself for that. So I keep scrubbing.

At the beginning you try everything to banish the thoughts from your life. You want things to go back to normal. The illness is the parasite and you are the whole original creature. Every moment is a battle to purge yourself of it and one day if you're smart enough strong enough therapised enough or I dunno Googled-up enough, you'll conquer it and reflect back on its corpse drifting away behind you. But after enough time—I'm talking years—you slowly begin to open your mind up to the dreadful possibility that the thing isn't going away after all. In fact it's been with you for so long that it's found increasingly clever ways to wheedle into cracks and crevices you didn't even know were there. The roots grow deeper, stronger, more numerous. It's impossible to imagine life without it; it's everywhere and in everything. You stop hoping for a future where things go back to normal and start to wonder: what does a future look like with this thing always beside me? Originally unimaginable and unacceptable. But if it's here to stay, surely I'd better find a way to live with it sooner or later, otherwise I'll have spent all my best years waiting for a victory that will never come, and you can't get those years back. And so it stops being a parasite and starts being something more like a new organ. You know, if your appendix could sing horrendous *Glee* covers in your ear 24/7.

The point is, in that beginning battlefield stage—like where I was when this started, back in 2013, back with Helene—you think that it might be the best idea to just abandon all attempts at relationships until you can conquer the beast. Then and only then will you finally be resolved enough to pursue something happily and in peace. But the battle drags on and on and on for long enough that eventually you're forced to consider what was before unthinkable: bringing it with you into a relationship. The world's most horrifying threesome.

But who oh who could I ever tell about these thoughts?

And who would ever love me once they knew?

## Toni

I stayed celibate like that for a long time. I made the decision with bleeding hands way back in that old mouldy mustard-coloured sharehouse to abandon sexuality completely until I had found a way out of the thoughts. Of course, they didn't go away, only dulled a bit, slowly, over time. Maybe I started to get a bit desensitised to them. Maybe it was the meds and therapy starting to work. In any case, by the time I managed to try dating again, I had forbidden myself any stimulation at all for a year and a half—imagine being that tense (any Catholics in the house?)—and I still wouldn't bring myself to masturbate for five more years (seriously where are my Catholics at?). An OCD specialist would say this was all avoidance and was making me sicker, but I still have no regrets. Sometimes you just need to sit out a few rounds, hey.

I make jokes about it now, but I've got to emphasise how absolutely fucking heartbreaking it is, what this illness has stolen from me over the years. I wanted nothing more than to just live life and enjoy my twenties like everybody else. To grow confident and have fun and challenge myself. To move around and learn things and date folk and explore my body and you know the rest. The most basic things, and OCD took it from me, all of it, in ways that I'm still fully realising today. What a burden for someone to carry: to think you're evil, while knowing you're not. This illness literally kills people, and you can see why.[1]

After that year and a half of celibacy, I managed to get just well enough to try dating again. My new partners' reactions to my obsessional fears—the ones I told them about anyway—varied across the spectrum from being understanding to confused to occasionally kind of cruel. I myself remained pretty overwhelmed and confused, more or less in a constant state of distress, desperately trying to find ways to convince myself to inch bit by bit, further and further out of the box I'd locked myself in, while at the same time being screamed at by my brain to stay safe in the goddamn box! I wanted to explore my sexuality while at the same time being pathologically terrified of my own sexuality. Riddle me that one. I even clumsily tried to experiment with polyamory once, with pretty disastrous results. In retrospect maybe going straight from celibacy to polyamory wasn't the best transition to try.

And throughout all of this, the obsessions still hounded me. But I wasn't alone on my bathroom floor anymore; once there was another person in the picture, my responsibility only multiplied, the potential consequences so much worse. The only solution to these extreme fears was to respond equally extremely.

I'd be repulsed by physical intimacy unless I felt 'clean': when one particular partner hugged her cat and then me, my brain would scream—while I tried to act normal of course. I was constantly hyperaware of everyfuckingthing that touched everyfuckingthing, seeing the world through shit-coloured glasses, while of course knowing it was all absurd and desperately trying to convince myself *not* to see it! I'm not crazy[2] okay. It was a constant tug-of-war in my own head. And contamination was only one thing.

---

1. People with OCD are ten times more likely to die by suicide than the general population: nature.com/articles/mp2016115.
2. I'd say I'm like fifty per cent crazy.

Over the years I'd also become increasingly obsessed with consent. I wouldn't want to hug or flirt with a girlfriend who'd had one more drink than me, or even one drink *full stop*; I couldn't even *touch* her if I was having the remotest doubts about our relationship—that would mean I was hiding something, *lying*, and even by hugging her hello I was violating her. Some links were even more obscure: I remember being alone in my parents' kitchen one night struggling to eat the last biscuit without asking because it might train my subconscious into taking things without consent and ... you see what I mean. I was hypervigilant of my potential to do the wrong thing at every moment, and haunted by the times before this when I hadn't had the same standards. Anything less than this and I was a rapist, an abuser, someone who liked doing more unspeakable things to cats than Andrew Lloyd Webber.

Perhaps this seems ridiculous, but believe me the risk felt as real and as possible as ever-so-slightly balancing the wrong way off a cliff. Once during this time I straight-up asked a partner if she found it annoying how much I asked for consent during sex. She said yes without much of a beat. I simply didn't know what to do. I was just trying to figure out *what was normal*, what was right (and of course plenty of things that are normal aren't right!). How on Earth do regular people navigate this stuff? *How do other people manage to be in relationships at all?!* How does anyone ever let go? There must be a way; millions of idiots do it every day. I don't think I'm an idiot, but I guess I am crazy.[3] Maybe I don't even want a relationship at all. Maybe I can't.

After being on-again-off-again with one particularly under-standing partner, I eventually ended it for good because the pressure of it all was just getting too much. It was me, not her—literally. I concluded, 'I just don't think I'm ready for a relationship.'

She responded bluntly: 'I don't think you are either.'

I once interviewed a Buddhist monk on the outskirts of Bendigo (move on, we don't have time) who had a sobering warning about

---

3. Okay, let's call it sixty per cent.

relationships. During his training in Tibet he'd been in love with a woman, and his lama (I said *move on*) told him he could certainly try to pursue things with her, but he was setting himself up for failure. And why do relationships so often not work? Well, *instead of one crazy mind, you've got two crazy minds,* he was told with a shrug. Basically, he could pursue either love or enlightenment. Those were two opposing choices. Well, enlightenment be damned, lama, because I was about to meet that second crazy mind.

'I have that, too,' she half-yelled over the bar noise.

'What do you mean?' Maybe I misheard her. You start to tell enough people about your OCD and you find out that *everyone* has it. I was wary and assumed this was another one of those.

'I have OCD, apparently. Diagnosed when I was put in a psych ward back in school.' Well shit.

Toni and I had hardly talked before this; we were working on the same little show but it wasn't until the whole crew went for commiseration drinks on closing night that we actually exchanged more than a couple of sentences, in this alleyway bar made of kerbside furniture and bric-a-brac. We spent the whole night talking. Everyone else left and they closed the roller door. We moved bars. She eventually crashed on my couch.

I knew she was special pretty quick. She was creative and goofy, liked to talk about risky weird shit and was a dreamer, too, like me. She was twenty-one to my twenty-six (my paedophile alert started screeching—*don't laugh, yes really*); OCD probably would have sent me running if it weren't for everything else. I'm glad I didn't listen to it this time.

Her OCD wasn't like mine though. Truth be told at that point she was doubtful she actually had it. Ain't that the way: everyone without OCD swears to high heaven they have it and the people actually with it think they don't. OCD has the sneaky habit of making you fundamentally doubt whether it's really there, even after diagnosis, even after you've been living with it for years. *Maybe it's not a mental illness and my thoughts are true after all?* The intrusive thoughts mimic real thoughts so well; they take up residence at the fringes and in the grey areas, morphing and dodging and transforming so easily that often it's hard to tell the difference.

This is not to mention that so many abstract obsessional questions can't be answered for certain by anyone, so who's to say if it's OCD or not? When does a regular belief in fate become a magical belief that abstract events are linked—something common in OCD? Is something like prayer (normal) really that different to saying a phrase three times to stop a bad thing happening (dysfunctional)? What about the growing appreciation for meditation—religious or otherwise—as an actual therapy? And who gets to decide which things are legitimate and which parts are disorder? Toni and I would talk about this stuff a lot. Her mind was much more open than mine.

I felt more comfortable around Toni than I ever had around anybody. We were very similar, and I mean that in every good and bad way. Everything that was hard with everybody else was suddenly easy and almost automatic with her. It very quickly felt like she'd been in my life for ages. Which is nonsense of course—I didn't believe in that shit any more, right? *That's some romantic French quiche bullshit, that is, Martin. You should know better by now.*

Saying I loved her was easy too. It just fell out one night, half-asleep. She said it back right away and that was that. The surprise was more that I didn't worry about it. I'd already made up my mind. There was no hair-pulling or soul-searching here. It was obvious: I loved her. Of course I did. Move on. To not torture myself over it was a cool relief after years of twisting.

For the first time I got to experience what it was like being on the other side of a relationship with OCD. *That'll teach me, right?* Suddenly I wasn't the only self-obsessed morally tortured one whose fears steered everything. You might think that this would make it impossible for us to do anything at all together, and let me tell you: yes. Absolutely yes. But it also meant we were speaking the same language. We didn't need to ask why or argue if suddenly one of us recoiled or paused or did something wacky. We recognised the look of fear in each other's eyes and that was enough. When stuck on a thought, sometimes our eyes would meet and we'd burst out laughing, like you just caught a glimpse of yourself in the mirror. That happens a lot with OCD actually: you have these sudden moments of self-awareness where you instantly pivot from a state of extreme fear and pain to … well, hysteria almost. *I mean, look at yourself.* Look at what you're doing. It is pretty funny. Toni and I saw it in each other every day.

But our OCDs were very, very different. She always used to walk on the side of the footpath closest to the traffic, in between me and the cars. She'd swap with me quickly if she found herself on the wrong side. I never knew why. Asking someone with OCD what they just had an intrusive thought about is like asking a prisoner what they're in for: it's just not done—and if they don't respond you definitely don't want to know.

I knew some of her thoughts were violent. Perhaps she felt a momentary impulse to push me into a speeding car. Perhaps the image of my crushed skull flashed in front of her eyes each time she was behind me. Perhaps it was some unexplainable weird combination of something her mum said once and a movie she saw that traumatised her and also the colour shirt I was wearing on the day and the way the sun cast a shadow of a tree in the shape of a dick-and-balls across my face (okay, that last one was mine). I really don't know what it was. But I tell ya, I really—*really*—didn't care.

See, we were the only ones who didn't judge each other's horrible obsessions. We both hated our own cloudy, confusing thoughts and were ensnared by them all the time, but we saw each other's with crystal clarity.

One day I worked from home in the morning, upstairs in the living room. When I came back to my bedroom a couple of hours later I found Toni there in more or less the same position I'd left her, sitting on a beanbag in the corner, arms clutched around her knees. I later learned that she'd frequently be stuck somewhere while I was stuck somewhere else, us both trying to do what we needed to do before we felt safe enough to see each other. She told me about one day she'd sat in her car on the street trying to convince herself to come inside, and when she did, she found me at the sink, washing my hands obsessively before she arrived. Our worlds were in matched orbit; maybe our mental illnesses were syncing, which is … romantic, I guess? Oh well. You work with what you've got.

But that didn't mean it was easy. Hell no! Toni and I are the same poles of two magnets: we could never really perfectly meet. We weren't two sides of the same coin, we were more like the same side of two coins, always knocking heads.

For the majority of the time we spent together we chose not to have sex too. Fuck that, with her my OCD was too much— and that suited hers just fine too, I think. So we lived a strange emotion-only relationship, meeting each other's families, even sleeping in the same bed, but no funny business. How on Earth do I keep getting more atheist yet keep acting more Christian?

She was only back in town for a short time, though, saving money to move to London and study. After a few months she left, pursuing those dreams that I never had the courage to properly.

I know, sorry to build you up just to let you down like that. It's true: she left my life as quickly as she arrived. I talk a big game about taking risks, but Toni is far more courageous than I'll ever be. When she was eighteen she'd spent a year living in France *by herself*; I spent a few days in France when I was twenty-two and all I got was the shits. Of course she was never going to stay back in Brisbane; and not I, or mental illness, or anything else could hold her.

Memories of Toni hovered over me for the years that followed, though, and still do. Over that time she and I went through peaks and troughs of contact, video chats and even a couple of visits. Eventually we stopped saying 'I love you', too—bit awkward to explain that to her new boyfriend over there. I never knew what to call her to my new partners either; I settled on my *special friend* in London. She's definitely much more than a friend but also definitely not a lover … what do you call that? She's closer to family maybe, but if I say that my incest alert starts screeching—*don't laugh, yes really*. In the end it doesn't really bother me what we call each other. But no, she's not *The One*. Sorry. By the end of this, I'm not sure if I'll even tell you which of these Loves I ultimately end up with.

Wouldn't this story be a whole lot easier to read if I had just one True Love? Wouldn't it be a whole lot simpler? God knows it'd be easier to write. That sounds familiar, hey: I could have a muse who haunted me throughout the years, a singular unrequited Love who I compare all others by, who I frame in these pages from the beginning to be the main character's primary love interest, and despite all the twists and turns and fights and flings along the way, we all know they're going to end up together. We're reading this to come along for the ride, but we can trust the safety restraints of the story. It doesn't matter what happens along the way, the ball's already been lobbed and it's soaring towards its inevitable landing place in the safe hands of *that person*. The ending is expected and inevitable, and the journey to get there was necessary—even fun.

We know these things even if we don't consciously *know* them, because we've seen it in stories thousands of times before. You know from the beginning who the main character is going to end up with: they're right there together on the poster, for crying out loud. I guess that's why people these days increasingly want to make their wedding videos look like sweeping big-budget cinematic romances and their photos like the poster. They're recreating the stories that they've seen and heard and envied their whole lives. They're playing the parts written for them. And it feels awesome and lovely. Despite all my cynical talk, *I* still do it—not even too different from that twenty-two year old with a bad quiche and a big heart.

## 2015, still on the fucking bathroom floor

I keep feeling like I've cleaned it enough, but the thought that there are still remnants of my piss/fluids here keeps coming back.

It jabs the middle of my mind like a hot poker, each moment of relief thinking I'm finished only there a short while before another inevitable wave of *ah, but what if?*

It's not just the general feeling of uncertainty, though. It feels much more real and immediate than that. Almost like I can 'see' the stains on the floor amongst the suds, but in my mind's eye. I can know they are there in a way that no microscope ever could. Even if a microscope could tell me there was absolutely no trace of anything left, perhaps it still wouldn't be enough. I've seen those crime shows with the black lights.

But it's not just the physical contamination that keeps me scrubbing. It's also to do with the number of times I scrub—I can't finish on an immoral number otherwise I have to start again. The thoughts seem poisonous to each other: they can't be allowed in my brain at the same time. The way I'm scrubbing matters too. Each time I scrub in a certain direction my brain punches me with the thought that I'm pushing my sexual germs out, further, north, south, east or west, in the direction of family members, neighbours' animals, schools in the area, everything even far beyond the horizon. I see shapes form in the suds on the floor: a circle or a bubble is the entrance to a vagina, a long stroke of the brush is a penis shaft. Each time I choose to keep scrubbing I need to erase them from the floor. So you see, the floor doesn't just need to be clean—it needs to *feel* right at the same time. Living with any of these things without trying to erase or redo them would mean I *wanted* them in my head, that I was okay with them staying there. Nobody would ever know—but I would.

*Because what really separates you from a pervert or a rapist or a murderer, Martin?* We like to think the difference is huge and fundamental, chalk and cheese. It's obvious. They are 'other'. Before their crimes were outed they were just pretending to be normal, and now finally they've been discovered, a sobering warning to the rest of us that there are other secret psychos among us right now just waiting for the same opportunity. There is something fundamentally different about people who do those things, call it whatever: evil, perverted, sick, criminal, psychopathic—it's unchangeable and unfixable.

*What if the more scary thing is true?* Maybe we all aren't that different from each other. These hands typing this right now could go strangle my housemate after I finish this sentence. There is absolutely nothing stopping me. But I don't, because I don't want to.

Ah, but there's the rub: how do I *know* I don't want to?

What do you believe about human nature? Do you believe it exists more consciously, where everything is choice, and we can essentially turn our shameful desires on and off? Or is it more base, lingering dormant deep in our subconscious ready to lash out if it decides in one moment it wants its desires fulfilled? Chimps are our closest genetic relatives and they'll eat your face off in a rage. What's the difference between us? Where is that difference? In our brains? In our 'souls', or whatever you want to call it? And have we truly lost the face-eating impulse or just smothered it in culture and language and religion and Mozart or whatever? Does the chimp still exist in you somewhere, deep down?

Tomorrow morning my housemate will be waking up early to go for a run. One of those community fun run things in a park. I imagine him walking through my piss blissfully unaware. I imagine his sneakers coated with my fluids out there, spreading them all around the park. I imagine who else will run there. Families, animals, any other adult who would have no idea I let him smear my stuff all over them, that I stood by and let it happen. When I could have taken action now. When I could've taken the effort to scrub this off the floor properly now. *When my housemate gets up tomorrow...*

I didn't know it then, but this was the worst my compulsions would get. Slowly I'd push myself in therapy, the medication would uncloud my brain and things would eventually get better than this. Not cured, as you've seen, but better. Much better.

I look up through the thick mottled glass at the grey silhouettes of trees starting to fade into view. This needs to finish. The sun is starting to come up.

## Katrina

Honestly, fate is a bit of a douche, I'd like to speak to the manager please. It was 2017, I had burned through all my savings on hand sanitiser long ago, and even though I wasn't having four-hour showers any more, I still wasn't working enough to live. It was quite inconvenient that, right then, almost exactly as soon as I moved back in with my parents, I met a bright, curly-haired wonder whose mere presence in my life would probably push me more than anybody else had. I say it was inconvenient but of course it was closer to poetically perfect: that living with my (amazing, generous, but more or less traditional) parents coincided with my first proper non-monogamous relationship. That's something you just don't bring up at family dinner.

We met at a party and somehow got talking about the *essence of table* or some nonsense. *What makes a table a table? Its intent? Its shape? Its usefulness?* Dear God, somebody time travel and put us out of our misery. Look, to be fair she had more reason to be talking about the essence of table than the idiot in front of her: she actually had a philosophy degree. Fuck, she was smart: could run rings around me, I loved it.

I saw Katrina for the longest I've ever been with someone, although even in that time we were never officially dating in the classic sense. She called us *lovers*, which I'd never thought of before but I really liked; it sounded like the perfect cross between free-spirited hippie and 1990s New York divorcee couple.

When we would kiss and I had an intrusive thought about her mane of curls, I would sharply pull my hand away. 'Oh that's right, I forgot,' she'd say, smiling. 'My hair is spiders.' She was very understanding of my sudden moments of disgust or out-of-the-blue yoyo-ing between affection and rejection. She would tell me when it hurt.

But by mistake, I'd finally found the perfect way out of my relationship obsessions: don't be in a relationship! It was like a cheat code. I suddenly wasn't worried about every minor thought, every minor doubt, and each momentary (and totally normal) feeling of annoyance or lack of attraction towards her wasn't heralding that we weren't 'meant to be together'. We weren't together! We'd both agreed. There was no pressure for the relationship to last forever so the fear that it would end evaporated. I'd found a way out of that particular obsession, and honestly it was such a relief. She'd tell me about guys who asked her out or a girl she went on a date with, and I would, um ... well I was open to it happening to me as well okay!

We are all saturated with the idea that there is a soulmate for each of us. Even if you aren't religious and don't have a spiritual connection to the idea, it's usually still the default setting for some reason. How many secular weddings have you been to where the bride marvels at having found her Best Friend, her Person, or the groom says he can't wait to grow old together with his SoulMate™? Even throwing around words like 'forever' in the vows is almost automatic, even among people who don't believe in forever at all. Why do we do this? Why do we believe this? I wonder how many people are simply on autopilot. Oh how much we think we know about the big-L Love, we actually take for granted. I didn't have to worry about any of that with Katrina. We were simply enjoying each other's company in the moment, and it was good—damn it was good. It was good and it wasn't forever. Why is that not just as legitimate a form of love?

That said, Katrina and I were fundamentally very, very different people. I was often puzzled why on Earth she wanted to hang out so much with stiff-necked, clenched-jawed, anxiety-ridden me. She was free and wild and energetic and warm and if you compare her to a manic pixie dream girl, she'll wanna have words with you, okay? She was sort of how I wished I could be. In fact, on the inside I saw myself that way already, and I ached to let it out but wasn't allowed. The obsessions boxed me in, creaking like old wood under growing pressure. She was wide open.

In a lot of ways, this kind of person was almost the opposite of what OCD required. Katrina wasn't structured, or neat, or private, or conservative. The world wasn't full of risk for her, it was full of possibilities. She would walk around barefoot and I would pick her up from festivals where she wouldn't shower for a week. If I was to picture a person that would piss off my OCD the most, she wouldn't be far off. We sure got on each other's nerves sometimes. In any case, she certainly wasn't *The One*. A more optimistic person might say that she—being exactly who she was—came into my life exactly as planned; for a reason.

Why do we assume that our Person comes to us either via fate or chance? *Thank you, Universe, for bringing this person into my life; what are the chances that of all the billions of people on the planet I crossed paths with one so perfect for me?* Isn't it more likely that we choose the relationship we were already looking for?

I still see Katrina every now and again; last I heard she was living on a property in the hinterlands growing cacao with her new partner. Good for her, I reckon—for a long time she would tell me about her dreams of living that kind of life, and now she's found someone who fulfils it. The more cynical part of me wonders if maybe this new partner represents something greater to her: a value, a dream, a desire that she had already decided long before she met him. But isn't that exactly what I do?

Did I really love that American in Cannes or did she just match close enough to the dream girl I'd already imagined up long before I met her? Did I truly love Toni or was it just that I was looking for someone who she fits snugly enough into the role of, and then the edges where she didn't quite fit I can stuff in and make feel close enough?

I wonder if it's the same thing with people who believe in *The One*. They'll ignore serious flaws in the relationship because they already believe this person is their other half, fated and ordained by God or Richard Curtis or someone. Their partner's bad qualities are easily dismissed because the value, the belief, the hope for the dreams they fulfil is so much stronger. We want so much for our dreams to be true. How much reality does that make us conveniently ignore? My grandparents were awful to each other but they were married their whole lives. Virtually all my memories of their relationship are of arguments and verbal abuse. I don't see how they loved each other, but I guess divorce was just *not done* for nice people of their generation, more so between a priest and the daughter of a bishop. (I will also never know if they had OCD, but my grandmother used to keep all the dishes separate at Christmas and they would bring their own bedsheets if they came to stay at ours.)

That's what I wonder: whether it's my Anglican grandparents or free-spirited philosopher-hippie Katrina or introverted, stifled, mentally ill me, maybe love isn't actually that complicated and we can just choose to find it if we're looking for it.

But how do we know we love the real person for who they actually are rather than our romantic imagination of them? If we will inevitably find the thing we're looking for simply because we're looking for it, then what am I looking for now? Can I change the thing I'm looking for? Will my irrational romantic dreams even let me?

Look, this is verging on self-help book territory so let's get back to the mental illness shall we (although those often go hand in hand).

## 2021

When I started writing this whateverthisis, I suddenly remembered that study I'd read about online years ago linking the brains of people in romantic love to people with OCD. At the time I read about it, before I even had OCD, it was one of those interesting little pieces of clickbait on social media that I scrolled past and nodded at meaningfully: *My heartbreak was like a mental illness! How deep and dramatic, \*turns on Radiohead\**. I had no fucking idea obviously. Now, almost ten years and an actual mental illness later, I decided to go looking for the real study.

I found it. In 1999 researchers from the University of Pisa, Italy, studied the brain biochemistry of people in the first six months of romantic love (of course this was in Italy). Strangely, they found very low serotonin levels, eerily similar to the levels found in the brains of participants with, you guessed it, obsessive compulsive disorder. This seemed to suggest, they reckon, that the type of obsessive thinking that folk with OCD get stuck in is comparable to the type of infatuation people in love have with their partner. They even won an Ig Nobel Prize in Chemistry for the study, which I suppose makes it more funny-concerning than funny-ha-ha.[4]

This is how the Pisa study defined romantic love: (a) the love relationship had begun within the previous six months; (b) the couple had had no sexual intercourse and; (c) at least four hours a day were spent thinking of the partner. Now I've been in love and I've been obsessed; but by all three of those criteria I have been more in love with my OCD than with any partner.

Today when I hear people talk so confidently and casually about their other halfs who they plan to grow old with et cetera, I feel happy for them, I really do. I'm envious and amazed that anyone can truly feel that sure. At the same time, I can't help but wonder: are they lying? Are they lying to the world? Or worse: to themselves? I'm gobsmacked, really. How is it possible to feel that way? I just can't imagine *ever* being *that* sure about *anyone*. I could have been once maybe, high on the smell of fresh pastry, but not anymore, not now.

But maybe all these things I'm describing—all these doubts, all these thoughts, all these mixed uncertain feelings—are what everyone else is experiencing all of the time too, even those blissfully happy couples on altars, but they just don't talk about it. I wonder if maybe these doubts are actually normal, common, inevitable, but I am just reacting to them more acutely. Maybe I'm

---

4. Asking someone like me to critically review a scientific journal is like asking an oyster to climb out of your bucket: no matter how hard I try I'm still gonna get eaten alive. So I crowdsourced some blink reactions: turns out a lot has happened in the world of neuroscience since 1999, and the Pisa study's conclusions might be a long bow to draw. But that's for someone else to talk about. I'll just cherrypick for poetic effect, thanks.

just more sensitive to the heat. Maybe my dial is just turned up. When I say that out loud, I realise I'm literally describing obsessive compulsive disorder.

And of course, everything you've read here is not the full story either. There are things from these years that I can only vaguely refer to because there's simply not enough time to go into it. This is meant to be specifically about OCD and relationships after all. But understand that it's not that simple; the effects of this fucking illness bleed and overflow from one aspect of your life into another until it's all mushed together in a weird thought soup and it's impossible to separate one struggle from its effect on another, one obsession from its link to another. Love has to do with commitment which has to do with family which has to do with career which has to do with purpose which has to do with fate which has to do with religion which has to do with morality which has to do with politics and Jesus Christ I haven't even mentioned sex yet. It's all tangled up together in a messy web of thoughts, emotions, memories, smells and pop songs.

Back when I was on my hands and knees in that collapsing sharehouse bathroom, scrubbing my invisible predatory sex germs off the floor, afraid I was a deep, dark, repressed pervert, I thought that any kind of love after this mental illness was *impossible*. Even if I got better somehow and it turned out that I was miraculously convinced the thoughts were untrue; good for me, but who would ever want to love me knowing that the thoughts had even existed in my head at all? It would be so much easier for any future first date to kick this fucked-up, lanky, blond kid to the kerb and go date someone with dark eyebrows instead of dark obsessions, and never have to deal with it. I felt tainted forever, and not even recovery could save me. But I was wrong.

Remember how I said Fate is a douche? Well it gets worse, and I'd like to speak to the manager's manager, please. You see, throughout the time it's taken me to write this piece all about love and OCD, I've coincidentally (or not) been in the best, most loving relationship for my OCD I've ever experienced. Ugh. How inconvenient. What makes it even more inconvenient is how truly wonderful Jordan is. I've told her everything about my OCD— more than any one of these partners I've written about here—she hasn't blinked: she's patient, kind, understanding, tolerant, curious and strong. I'm trying to be a tortured artist here. What a bitch.

How strange, to be writing and reflecting about years long in the past, trying to forcibly mould a final solid story out of already mushy memories, while at the same time being thrown new chunks of memories that you have no idea where they fit. How can I confidently put any of these things to paper if they keep wanting to be rewritten?

I started out this journey, long before OCD, before any relationship at all, dreaming of that one perfectly imperfect Love who was my other half, and who, whether I admitted it out loud or not, was that girl from my dreams. It would be so easy to say that this relationship now—for sure the best of them—is finally the end of the story, and where all these flings and fights and heartbreaks have been leading. Of course there is no journey except when you look back; there is no story except the one you decide to write down; there is no romantic arc that leads you inevitably to where you are meant to be in the arms of your eternal Ryan Gosling; and there is no ending at all.

I could try to craft any manner of romantic narratives about me and Jordan on these pages now. I could plant the seed with our meet-cute, a whole year before even getting together; how we stood silently next to each other at a gig for half an hour without saying a damn thing; how one year later on New Year's Eve we both conspired, independently, to make sure we were at the same mutual friend's party. I could go on and on with cute stories, marvelling at Fate's cheeky puppetry. It's a romantic story and one that could easily fit the dream if I wanted it to. And part of me does want it to.

Even now; even after all this; even after a bad quiche and a panic attack; even after the deepest dark and the cleanest floor; even after bleeding hands and years as a neuter; even after heartbreak and confusion and medication and therapy; I *still* have that timid little flame burning in me, hoping, dreaming, meekly looking out for that singular, transcendental, romantic Love just like in the movies. Even after everything, I still have to catch myself. Maybe I will never let myself fall again.

Fate gets talked about a lot with Love. But this concept of Fate —the illusion of some grand control, some beautiful choreography making things just as they should be—is actually anathema to good treatment for OCD, which requires you to accept the exact opposite: the true randomness and chaos of life. Both cannot be true. These obsessional years have painfully dragged me kicking and screaming from one belief to the other, forcing me to let go and scattering me wildly and haphazardly in a way that can never be put back together. But that's really how I prefer it.

Obsessions all come from a place of love, true, but it's the kind of love that's dysfunctional and unhealthy. So how do you know the difference? Real love requires letting go some, allowing room for the real unplanned joy and pain to bleed in and fill the gaps. Obsession doesn't tolerate that breathing room. It alone is enough to fill you. It demands more than any partner would.

One night recently I kissed Jordan goodnight and caught a glimpse of the time: it was on a bad number. Fuck. I felt the immediate familiar sting, the tighten, the scrunch of my eyes. My OCD desperately wanted to redo it, just a minute later, just when it was on a good number, just to make the pain go away and bring me back to ground and have everything make sense again.

Knowing it was a compulsion, Jordan refused. She understood what my OCD still doesn't.

# Filthy but Fine:
# OCD and T&A in NYC

Patrick Marlborough

*Dedicated to the 53M8s and the L train:*
*may the next stop be yours.*

Sane people are dud roots. It's one of life's sadder truisms. Sane people fuck like they're laying out a picnic blanket: unfold, whip it out, sit on it, fold it back up, place it in the basket, tuck it back in the boot to be brought out next time the weather's nice. Sane people are terribly tedious and we see that in their lives, their art, and of course, their sex. It's hell to live amongst them as a tourist/ hostage. As a nutter, etc. Us mad folk must suffer in the big asylum they call 'society,' pumping ourselves with prescription uppers and downers that make us as limp and as frisky as them—mainlined protestantism on behalf of the erstwhile savages. To be mad, and in treatment, is to go through a gauntlet of chemical castrations, specially designed to cut the chronic masturbators and dry humpers who are having too good a time off at our carpet-burned knees.

Such is the fate of the horndog in the Land of the Sane, serfs in the Kingdom of the Dud Root.

Australia, for all its meanness, is a desperately sane place. We are filled to the brim with cruelty, despair, and suicide, but it runs on an incredibly level-headed and cool logic that's as clinical as it is rehearsed. Nothing mad about it, in the proper sense. We are decisively sane. Just look at our literature, the majority of which spends its time gargling on about middle-aged frumps returning to their hometowns to have an epiphanic moment of self-discovery amongst the tawdry gossip of the mortifying lower-middle classes: a grand trauma dredged-up, a middle-aged creative writing tutor's affair with a 19yo student, our bodies in spaces and how those spaces make our bodies relate to said spaces and on and on ad infinitum. Dull dull *dull*, and all terribly sane.

Australia is the primary vassal state of the Kingdom of the Dud Root. We fuck like a country that's watched too much rugby: meaty repetitive thumping, all towards a simple singular goal. And, like a rugby player, our national sexuality has taken on late-stage CTE. We're dribbling on ourselves, and lashing out. Good sex requires pride in imagination, pride in empathy, pride in experimentation, and an ability to embrace one's shame. Nothing terrifies Australia more than these rather basic notions. And so, we fuck like we are stuck living in the Howard years—as if we were Peter Costello, forever waiting our turn.

*Dull.*

Perth, where I'm from, is as erotic as a licensing centre. People who say 'but ah, what about our beautiful beaches?' have obviously never had sex on one. No, Perth has all the sensuality of the mining sector that it loves so much. Dig a hole, fill it in. Dare us to dream beyond that and you're asking for trouble.

*Well if ya don't like it, leave* is a refrain I've heard my whole life (heck, you might be thinking it right now, dear reader) so I'm here to tell you upfront: I did.

As I got further into my twenties, I could feel myself getting, well, *nuttier*. I collected diagnoses like they were Pokémon cards: anxiety, depression, bipolar 2, ADHD, high-functioning autism, and of course, my OG, good old OCD. Who can tell where one ends and another begins—to me, it's simpler to bundle them all up into the bindle of 'wacko' and carry on my merry way. So I did just that. Perth began to feel like a padded cell, so I bit a nurse and made a runner for the only place I'd ever felt anything close to *sanity*:

Bedlam. The Nut House. Da Big Apple.

New York City.

Well, a loft apartment above a working glue factory in Bushwick, Brooklyn, to be specific.

## DSM DMs

This is an anthology about OCD, so I suppose I should stop and explain it and what it is to me. But, due to my varying mental disorders (see above), I do find the prospect of doing so sort of ... tedious? Don't get me wrong, I've fattened my purse (see: been paid slightly below the minimum wage) turning my trauma and my illness and my disability into grist for the mill of some of the world's biggest content spewers; that said, however, I'm not sure I entirely subscribe to the efficacy of this practice, in terms of enlightening the unafflicted, and raising that dreaded ghoul called 'awareness'. I do not trust the sane's ability to fully grok the actualities of being nuts, nor do I pretend that my fellow nutters fully agree with any one telling of their particular brand of nuttiness. I'm always left asking 'who is this for?' and I'm always left thinking 'a substitute teacher somewhere', which is, to me, a very disheartening thought.

My big problem with writing about madness is that it's often written for the benefit of the sane, translated into their tongue and onto their terms in a way that helps them pat themselves on the back, or at least throw out some factoid as a bit of banter at one of their interminable dinner parties. I don't like giving them any more of me than they've already taken, to be frank (hi Frank, I'm autistic!).

But I promised to write about having OCD and living in NYC, so I'm going to do my best to deliver. Which involves a lot of digression, because, as I've said, I'm quite mad. And anyone familiar with OCD knows that it is really a disorder *of* unwarranted and untamed *digressions*.

But I'll make it easy for you sane people and use diagrams so you can follow along.

Now, see figure 1 for an example of my OCD thought patterns, as a young, single Australian they/them/dog living in Da Big Apple:

*fig. 1:*

Obsessive thought is a bit like being stuck in traffic with a very angry ice-cream truck tailgating your rear bumper, honking its horn repeatedly while simultaneously blasting a demented rendition of 'Greensleeves'. An obsessive thought is a big ol' scab just begging you to pick it. It can take many shapes and many forms, some granular, some grandiose, and those find relief in what's called a 'compulsion' (I think; I admittedly zone out when my psychiatrist is talking).

Here's a relatively banal one: when I was a kid, I'd have to keep the pattern in the cracks in the sidewalk balanced. What I mean is: if I stepped over a crack (note: as in a dividing crack, not an accidental one) with my left foot, then I'd have to step over the next with my right. If the distance in cracks meant that I was making 3 lefts for every right, I would keep a mental note of that imbalance, and work to correct it as soon as the opportunity arose. This somehow led me to finding great comfort, and relief, in the number 5, which I came to see as a pattern fixer, of sorts.

A similar tic I had was tapping out a pattern with my hands or fingers. Right tap, left tap would have to be balanced with left tap, right tap—which itself would have to be balanced, leading to a sorta infinite little digit bongo session on my desk, which could only be broken when my teacher's patience finally snapped.

As an autistic, as *obsessive*, I frequently become *obsessed* with certain subjects. I never know what it's going to be in advance, nor do I really know why I settled on any one thing. As a teenager, it was pre-war American blues, folk, and country music. In 2018, the year I moved back to New York, it was Akira Kurosawa and Evel Knievel. When I was five it was dinosaurs, when I was nine it was Pokémon, when I was fourteen it was James Joyce. One obsession doesn't fade as the other revs up, rather they tangle and jumble, and collect like a big rolling ball of trash: a giant wobbling Jenga tower where each block, in some way, leads to and holds up another. All vital, in the intricately interlaced clockwork of my 'divergent' mind.

Where OCD comes in, I think, is in the more actionable obsessions. As a kid, I was terrified of shitting due to my overwhelming disgust at the very idea of toilets. In fact, I didn't once piss at school for my entire schooling: years one through twelve. And I used to drink a litre of Brown's ice coffee every lunch. Now *that* is crazy. Habits, routines, tics and triggers snowball. You find ways to bend and twirl around them but they inevitably catch you off guard, somewhere, at some point. Keeping them in check is exhausting, you see. You get tired. You get distracted. You let your shield down. Perth/Australia is so deadly for that reason: the place is so flat and empty and relatively quiet that any trigger/sore point sticks out like a swastika graffitied onto a Rothko.

You can't not notice.

Which is why New York—despite all its grit, grime, and muck— is so great for my particular brand of OCD. There is so much of everything that the noise, the mess, the people overwhelm me to the point that I zap out and achieve a state of zen. In the same way my psychiatrist gives me Nazi-grade speed to calm my thinking, an L train overflowing with burnt-out workers and lunatics helps me feel at *peace*.

In New York, your obsessions become discernible and, like I said, *actionable*.

## Gagging for It

My enduring obsessions are sex and comedy.

I think I watched too much *Sex & the City* as a small boy. Other than teaching me that freelance writing is the only viable career option for someone with a personality disorder, it also taught me that sex is funny. And I loved funny. Comedy was my first— and remains my longest lasting—obsession. And compulsion. I was sent out of class the morning of 9/11 for doing a five-minute stand-up set where I impersonated Kermit the Frog reporting on the towers coming down, as well as nailing a mean impersonation of Sesame Street's Count doing the body tally. I was ten years old. Goofing is one bad habit I cannot shake, one compulsion that has caused me more harm in my personal and professional life than all the others combined: the urge to be a smartass, above all else, is terminal.

I should make it clear now that being passionate about something is not the same as enjoying it. Being passionate to the point of obsession can often be its own agony, one rooted in an impossible quest for perfection and all knowingness, that can never truly be satiated.

I realised young that sex and comedy were intertwined when, at four, I traded a dirty joke for my first kiss (fun fact: she was the daughter of a very famous Australian author, who will remain unnamed, due to the 'tightness' of our literary community and the fact I can't stand his [very popular] work). That was a dangerous lesson: that it didn't matter what breed of puny weird looking freak you were, if you were funny, you could woo just about anyone.

Good comedy is a lot like good sex in that it's all about making a refined act look completely improvised. It's all about knowing your audience, and giving them what they want. (NOTE: do not read this and go out and have sex with a comedian. Comedians are second only to poets in terms of miserableness, selfishness, and tbh, bad rootery—being funny and being a comedian are two very different things, which, in my professional opinion, rarely meet.)

That said, there are exceptions, and lo and behold I had moved to New York as both a writer and a comedian, and a mad (literally) romantic. I was finally Carrie Bradshaw, minus the fifty-thousand-dollar shoes, and perhaps having consumed the soul, essence, and lust of Samantha for good measure.

It was time to find my Mr Big, and become him.

## Swipe Left at Lorimer

It's a little-known fact that the state verb of New York is swipe. The first action you must master as a new New Yorker is that of swiping your MetroCard at a subway entrance. It takes a while to get the casual yet assured flick of the wrist that's required to make the admittedly rather busted turnstiles read your card and let you on through. Hilary Clinton's presidential campaign was undone by a fifteen-second clip of her struggling to enter the New York subway. Donald Trump, quite wisely, has never stepped foot on it in his life. Once you get the knack of it and that awful *beep beep beep* hailing your ineptitude makes way for the heavenly *ca-clink* of the unlocking bars, then buddy, you're ready to ride the greatest public transport system of 1932! Take your seat; puddle of piss included free of charge.

The swiping I found myself doing on the train, in my apartment, and in my bed, was of another variety altogether, however. It was on Tinder. By the time I first moved to New York I'd been a Tinder habitué for some time. It had gamified my horniness and tapped into my obsessive habits more efficiently than a pokie machine that paid out blowjobs. Before Tinder, I was a dyed-in-the-wool *eyes meet across the crowded room* romantic/philanderer, but the little data-mining goblin app widened my horizons considerably. Through it, I met some of the best fucks, flings and friends of my life—which is strange to admit, as a natural-born, tech-adverse cynic.

But Tinder's efficacy is regional. Tinder in Perth is … well … let's just say I have too many cousins to make using the app in such a small city truly *enjoyable*. In New York, however, it is another beast entirely.

My first night in Brooklyn, after I'd become best friends with my roommate and settled into the punk-squat-factory-loft that would be my home on and off for the next three years, I began swiping, and I began matching. Matching with people who felt like they were cooked up in the bowels of Silicon Valley themselves: as if all the websites, all the apps, all the devices which had been spying on me since my early teens had collated all their information to present me with potential lovers who were exactly, eerily, my *type*. I'm talking leggy leggy, Italo-Idahoan, graphic designer ballbusters my *type*, or North Eastern, piano prodigy slash alt-hardcore singer-songwriter, Holly Hunter lookalikes my *type*, AND/OR smart-mouthed Jewish poetess communists with a kink for asthmatics, my capital T *type*. I felt like Augustus Gloop running through the chocolate factory, dunking my head in the big swirling pool of sugary lava and immediately drowning myself in the most perfect form of auto-erotic asphyxiation. *Bliss*.

Heaven.

Which is hell.

The thing about obsession is you can't turn it off, and the thing about compulsions is that you can't stop yourself. I have no trouble accepting rejection/nos (well, other than the very human 'ah dang' feeling we all get) but I do have a fair bit of trouble *saying* no, even to things I don't want. Because the scab *demands* to be picked, etc. As you can imagine this can lead to some difficulties, sad, humiliating or just outright harmful in the bedroom. I can be too accommodating, and too forgiving. Especially back in 2017, when I was manic and immature beyond my own comprehension and control.

Most of these incidents are, on paper, fairly banal. One I remember fondly involves a beautiful ad exec of Cambodian descent who I spent a couple of fun weekends with. When we matched on Tinder, I was at the big art/zine fair at MoMA PS1, and she was back at her lavish apartment in Greenpoint, just around the corner from where I was briefly crashing with my cousin and her partner an hour or so away on the G train. An hour or so later we were in bed together, introducing ourselves to one another. Her dad bred exotic fish, her mother was a refugee, she had just finished filming a Nike commercial featuring Serena Williams— y'know, pillow talk. We got to talking about sex and what it is we like, don't like, and what it is we fetishise. I always hate having this chat (on my end) because my kink is at best boring, at worst calculated, and worst again, from where I stand, wholly sincere: I get off on what the other person gets off on. A very 'your wish is my command' type of guy, which is good in ways and limiting in others—but I think my autism has allowed me to master the art of the chameleon, a skill/habit/tic/kink that has its place in the bedroom. Hers was something else, however. Something I'd never heard before:

— I like when people hurt themselves ...

Ok, I said, not really my bag: I can't do any form of violence to myself or others, consensual or otherwise. Just too much of a wimp (she was already made aware of this when she'd asked me to punch her in the face mid-act, and I had demurred.)

— No, no ... nothing like that. No, what I really like is well ... have you ever watched old episodes of *Star Trek*?

I had.

— Well ... you know when characters get shot or killed or whatever ... how they ... fall down?

I did.

— That ... that drives me wild. People just ... falling down like that.

I asked if she meant pratfalls. Surprisingly, she wasn't familiar with the term. We brought up YouTube and I typed in 'great slapstick pratfalls' and we watched a compilation of Buster Keaton, Charlie Chaplin, Harold Lloyd and the likes slipping on banana peels, cream pies, and conveniently placed rollerskates down stairs, over rails, and through walls to land laid out flat on their well-worn butts.

— Oh my god ...

She was *literally* drooling.

Have you ever had sex with someone so revved up by a clip of Buster Keaton falling down an elevator shaft that you felt like they might drop you down one yourself? Of course, when I was eighteen, Keaton became one of my autistic special interests, and

I became incredibly good at doing his deadpan forward flip ass drop. Never in my life did I think this Vaudevillian slapstick would get me so vigorously laid.

This was not the kind of gag I was used to in the bedroom.

Another date had me at a surreal bar in the Lower East Side, courting a lingerie designer/model with a thick Eastern European accent. I say the bar was surreal because its theme was *Australian*, which was why my date had requested to meet me there. Now, I'd experienced my fair share of Australiana kitsch in my travels throughout America (New York itself is riddled with 'Australian style' cafés [cafés that serve flat whites]), but most of them boiled down to the Outback Steakhouse mode of Crocodile Dundee/Steve Irwin chic. This was … something else. It was a perfect recreation of the kind of wood panelled green-carpeted mid-70s Australian suburban town house I associated with visiting my family's elderly Italian friends in the mid-1990s. Frighteningly—monstrously— there were framed portraits of Daryl Somers on the walls. I took this in with the growing sense that I had been lured into a trap, or perhaps into some parallel dimension, where Daryl Somers' tulpa was going to murder me and possess my corpse in some kind of demonic ritual. Instead, I was met at the bar by my date, who was wearing nothing but a loosely tied golden kimono and incredibly transparent lingerie, looking like something out of a classy porn parody of a Lazenby-era Bond film.

Ok, I thought, I am definitely getting murdered tonight but … what the hell!

We drank and necked, and by one in the morning (we had met at eleven) she told me if I could guess which country she was from, she would go home with me. I think I must have named every country in the Eastern Bloc bar the one she was actually from (Chechnya, btw). And I pride myself on accents, and my ability to pick their origin, like a poor man's Professor Higgins. My date had told me that the owner of the bar was Australian, which explained the terrifying fidelity to detail, and that that was him, working behind the bar. It was a bloke my age, maybe a few years older, a perfect Aussie in the true American fantasy sense: well-tanned, white-toothed, broad-shouldered—a stark contrast to my sandgroper Sméagol aesthetic. I said:

— If I can guess what *suburb* in Australia that bloke is from, will you come home with me?

— Sure, she said.

— Hey mate, I called out and he looked up, you from Bondi?

— Awww yeah, how'd ya know?

(I'll tell you how: if you're an immaculate thirty-one or so year old surfy Aussie guy who owns and operates a Daryl Somers themed bar in one of Manhattan's hippest suburbs, then your hereditary wealth and beachy athleticism places you in one of two townships: Bondi or Byron Bay. I just happened to guess right!)

Anyway, we took a circuitous cab back to my place in Brooklyn (she lived with her mother in Harlem) and gave the cabbie a show that probably raised our fare a fair bit. Then, back in my closet-sized room in my fume-filled loft in my illegal punk-squat collective apartment above a glue factory etc., we had sex that helped me finally appreciate the violent deterioration of the Soviet Union in full.

At some point she punched me, quite violently, in the nose which, tragically, made me laugh. My sparring partner mistook this laughter for me climaxing (let's not with that old cliché) and decided to slug me once again, barking 'don't come, man' in her incredibly thick accent, which, to my great shame, made me laugh even harder, which, of course, sparked another punch followed by what remains the funniest/worst/best thing anyone has ever said to me during sex:

*fuck me with your fat convict cock!*

I thank Christ for the paper-thin walls in my apartment, which ensured that my four roommates, plus my neighbour Jake, were able to hear and bear witness to this statement which, fate being kinder, would have been the final words I heard on this green earth and perhaps my epitaph. Definitely worth the follow-up punch, all the same.

I drag these kiss-and-tells out as cutesy little vignettes from a tapestry filled with repetitions, recapitulations, and relapses. There is a point where sex as habit—as compulsion—makes you feel a bit like a sentient dildo. You are the compassionate autistic—incapable of rage or anger or violence and all those things that make casual sex so dangerous for women (and men) everywhere—with a built-in level of untenanted compassion stemming from a lifelong inability to understand what it is that makes 'normal' people so so hateful, topped off with an obsessive artisan's approach to the act of fucking and romance, and topped off again with, what some have generously dubbed 'a fat convict cock'—you are a volunteer gigolo, slowly becoming locked into a role you can't break free of.

So you keep swiping. You keep matching. And you keep getting sucker-punched.

## A Pocket or Two

Oh, there is another form of swiping that I *should* mention. Another uncomfortable itch I have to scratch. The 'convict cock' is more astute than she could have known. That is to say: I am a thief, and a good one at that. Reams of scholarly hoo-ha has been written on the links between OCD and similar impulse control disorders like ye olde kleptomania, but I do hate to cheapen something so romantic with the drudgery of diagnosis. I steal because it's fun, and no one can stop me.

(DISCLAIMER: I am white. Do not attempt any of this at home if you are not—being white is the secret to getting away with all crimes, especially theft. Theft is the closest thing a white person has to traditional culture. If you aren't white, then you already know that we live to steal, sorry!)

Theft started as another one of my obsessions, before it became another one of my habits. As a kid, I was entranced by Oliver Twist, specifically Fagan and the Artful Dodger. Having mainly loved the 1968 musical *Oliver!*, and having skimmed over the part in the book where Fagan is hanged, I saw these two characters as a carefree blueprint to a life lived cheekily, if not criminally. I am the grandson of a cop and I am raised—cripplingly—to be a lawful person, so my theft never went further then pickpocketing and watch-undoing, all of which I'd return by the task's end, it essentially being little more than a parlour trick I did to kill time in class. But all my friends growing up were shoplifters, mainly by necessity (which I didn't share), and through them I got a second-hand education in how to make a packet of Maltesers, a DVD, or a pair of pants disappear.

I didn't start shoplifting habitually until my twenties, when my bipolar mania suddenly clicked into overdrive, and remained stuck there at a steady hum. The maniac fears nothing, and shoplifting is fairly low on the list of risks you are willing and able to take without a second thought while in that holiest of states. Plus, I seemed preternaturally gifted at it. Shoplifting is an act of illusion and, as an autist, I was highly skilled at being illusory: putting on the face of normalcy and sanity to navigate that big old Land of the Sane, constantly being two to ten people at once.

Plus, I had morals (haha). I never stole from independent stores. Nothing small, nothing local. Only big chains, nothing unique or sentimental, things that would be noticed only by stingy general managers working for companies that filled factories with slaves, cleared swathes of rainforest, and pumped whole villages' wells dry, all so they could make Minion merchandise and the likes for the baseline of some Moloch petroleum conglomerate.

Thief is the only honourable occupation under capitalism, and I see it as a gravely immoral act to not engage as one.

New York is a thief's city. From the old pickpockets and turnover men of the Five Points two-hundred years ago, to the robber baron coke-huffers of modern Wall Street, New York, like any jewel in the crown of a colonial empire, sits on a bedrock of larceny big and small.

In New York, my main targets were my absolute favourites: galleries.

There is nothing like being a *true* patron of the arts. The art gallery gift shop theft is one of the simplest, and one of the most romantic. You are surrounded by marked up gewgaws and trinkets, high on taking in the genius of history's greatest artists (all of them thieves in one way or another), thinking of who you'll be bedding tonight, and you're totally invisible: just another patron in a crowd that daily reaches into the hundreds of thousands. At one run at the Met, I stole over $800 worth of necklaces and silk kerchiefs, totally unfazed and unnoticed, totally in my element, totally carefree. My Christmas was sorted that year. A lot of lovers have gold necklaces and kerchiefs to remember me by.

In Australia, stealing from a gallery gift store can be seen as an act of cultural vandalism, our arts industry, being what it is, barely kept afloat by the sale of Frida Kahlo socks and Vincent Van Gogh magnets and the likes—a loss of $19.95 can spell ruin.

But in New York, the big galleries are kept afloat by literal war criminals (have you seen the Monet in the Lockheed Martin wing?), billionaires (history's greatest thieves), and a ketamine-addled oligarchy. These are quite literally the créme de la créme of the global elite: not to sound like a conspiracy nut, but it is hard to feel remorse while stealing from a place funded by the Koch brothers and Haliburton. Then there is the stark reality of galleries operating like a fence's display cabinet. As you walk around the Met—past the Greek statues, the Egyptian sarcophagi, the ancient African jewellery— you're struck by the realisation that a majority of the stuff you're looking at *was* pilfered. Every 'discovered by' is followed by the name of some early twentieth-century grave-robber. Not a gallery, but the American Museum of

Natural History is wall-to-wall animals shot, stuffed, and mounted by beloved warmonger Teddy Roosevelt, not to mention the harrowing collection of Indigenous people's skulls.

There's no honour amongst thieves, and I'd love Teddy Roosevelt to try to stop me from wearing a Natural History Museum hoodie straight out the front door and on past his fascistic statue. As for galleries: I do not think Georges Seurat—who died young, obscure, and penniless—would give two Sundays re me filling up on goodies for my friends and family at the Met gift shop. Georges Seurat is *dead*.

On our last Saturday in New York together in 2019, my French roommate Clarisse and I went on a touristy Christmas sojourn through Manhattan, stopping at Macy's and other sites that our long stints in New York had otherwise numbed us to. At each stop, I filled my coat pockets with a little bit of everything. Macy's is (allegedly) the hardest place in New York to shoplift from—they have a basement lockup for thieves, supposedly—but again, the crowds and my performative touristness made me just another face, stoked to see Santaland, in all its gargantuan gaudiness. American excess is the best disguise and the best excuse for theft, just ask Bernie Madoff. On the L train home, I opened up my pockets, and showered Clarisse with all the gifts I'd squirrelled away, totally unknown to her, even though I'd been standing right in front of her chatting away while pocketing things all day. She said:

— You are a magician. A poet!

Which lands especially hard in a thick French accent.

— It is very romantic. You are an artist. It is in your blood!

And maybe she was right. There is something about my Australianness—the fat convict cock etc.— that I lean into while in New York. Which is odd, because I was there to escape everything about my country (well, just its culture, history, government, and people) which broke my heart. But Americans see Australians as quasi-mythic figures, caught somewhere between Crocodile Dundee and Nicole Kidman. Although there are so many

Aussies in New York that it borders on being a refugee crisis for underemployed Aussie artsy types (and bankers, oddly), we still retain an air of exoticism. My American friends who had had the misfortune of meeting Australians while travelling—particularly through South-East Asia—are all too aware of the *Wake in Fright* chinless cronyism that makes up the large part of our national character, but luckily for me, few Yanks ever make it overseas, and continued to hold me in fascination.

You have a lot of conversations like:

— Australia: wasn't your country a prison colony? Isn't it full of criminals?

— Yes it was, of course, but only after your country stopped being one and decided it'd rather keep doing slavery than keep paying the British taxes. And don't you throw one in five of your citizens in prison?

— You don't have guns, right? What if a guy breaks into your home and steals your TV?

— I don't think I could shoot a man over a television. But the lack of guns does hit hard when I get the urge to camp out in a book depository waiting for the Prime Minister to drive by.

Chatting, I'd find myself leaning in to my twang, hitting the hard 'mates' and 'g'days' in ways I never would here, taking on the role of a Ben Mendelsohn styled 'awww yeaaah/ yeaaah/naaahh' Aussie charmer, a loveable antipodean scamp—an Artful Dodgy, if you will.

In that role, I could steal anything.

Theft, sex, and comedy all tickle that OCD urge to *perform*. To suffer OCD is to be adept at subterfuge. If you want to get by in this world—if you want to get laid—you have to hide the fact that you are, essentially, in a constant state of distress. Those tics and triggers never stop humming for me, and these compulsive acts—

the steal, the shag, the stand-up—offer brief islands of reprieve in what is otherwise an ocean of agony. In all three of these acts are invisible rules, patterns, and games that magnetise and soothe your hyper-focus, and keep you from thinking about picking up and licking the horrid dogshit* you stepped over three blocks ago.

These acts form habits, and you get stuck in them—be it swiping through Tinder for four hours without realising, or swiping a statue of the Virgin Mary at the Vatican gift shop (the old nuns working it are blind, to be fair)—you find yourself going through these actions with no real purpose or discernment all because you know if you stop, the electric sting of the unkempt thoughts hurtling round your head 24/7 will lay you flat.

So you fuck, you steal, you riff until that sting is buried, or at least defanged.

But it never really goes away.
   So you go on the lam, and lay low until the heat cools off.
   After all, a thief is only as good as their hideout.

## 53M8s

When the unlicensed taxi driver that funnelled me into his black SUV while I was in a sleep-deprived daze at the airport robbed me of my birthday money and dumped me outside 538 Johnson Avenue for the first time, I thought: *oh dear.* This was not your typical New York apartment building. You're met by a defaced and heavy front door, not a homely one, but rather one built for the workers of a factory to enter and exit—weighty, sad, efficient looking. This is of course because the loft apartment on the second, third and fourth storeys of the infamous 538 Johnson Avenue are above two working factories: one prints Hebrew Talmuds; the other makes what I have only ever heard described as an 'architectural industrial strength glue'. The exhaust pipe to the latter would run

---

* The question, 'is that human shit?', is one you'll ask yourself a lot in New York.

under my bedroom in the loft that would be my New York home whenever I was lucky enough to be there.

And in the years I came and went, it truly became my home.

Walking up the metal stairs, thick with ash trash, and ephemera, you're met by a hallway that is wall-to-wall—floor-to-ceiling— graffiti. When I first made that walk around midnight the day after my twenty-seventh birthday, people (my future neighbours) were in there, spray painting their tags and smoking. The hallway is often full of punk, hardcore, and scene kids of varying stripes and varieties. The neighbours across the way run a cult DIY noise venue out of their space, the others a kinda experimental art space. The one between them has a half-pipe built into it (we get a lot of late-night skaters on our roof). On Saturdays, Sundays, and heck, really any day of the week, I'd walk up the stairs with my bags of groceries to find five hundred or so blitzed-out rave goths standing around smoking their vapes, asking me where the toilets were, and offering me a hold of their Instagram-famous snake (it was a very nice snake, which I still remember fondly).

Our apartment was an oasis from all this, of sorts. My roommate Oscar had lived there for a decade or so when we first met. A musical genius of the first order, Oscar may be one of the only people I've met in this life that could swing a sainthood without converting to Catholicism. We became brothers in a week or so. Over the next three years, roommates from all over the world and from all walks of life would come and go, and they would all, for the most part, become a part of an incredibly close and loving family that we dubbed 'the 53M8s'.

That's not to say there aren't drawbacks to living above a working-glue factory. The place was (and is) a filthy deathtrap. I almost got cooked alive one summer when the factory exhaust pipe which snakes under my bedroom heated up the place like a pizza oven, causing the giant mancoon Apollo and I to almost perspire from heat exhaustion (I was saved by an Aussie painter I matched with on Tinder, matter of fact), and the fumes did leave me with a months-long bout of chemical pneumonia, an illness which, according to the lung specialist who treated me, 'essentially died with the Industrial Revolution'.

But I love 538 all the same, and it will forever remain my happy place.

It is hard, I'm sure you can imagine, to reconcile such a space with OCD. I'll admit, although my feline friend Apollo was incredibly dear to my heart, passing his litter box every day never failed to leave me with a case of the dizzies. The dust, the grime, the grit, etc. was everywhere, and I found myself having hypermanic cleaning episodes, like when I dismantled and deep cleansed the interior of the stove which hadn't been looked at since at least the mid-aughts, which is how Clarisse met me, funnily enough.

It was my first time really living with people—*strangers*. My various mental disorders had made it difficult for me to function back home, and had made it even more difficult for me to manage a task like moving out without becoming immensely overwhelmed and shutting down. Half the reason for my initial shift to New York was to force myself into an extreme state of flux and change that would force me to confront and break my OCD patterns. 538 was me jumping in the deepest of deep ends (unwittingly at first) but I think the absolutely hectic shambles it was always in allowed me a kind of mutability that a simpler place could not have brought out of me.

When I did find myself overwhelmed with sensory stimuli to the point of paralysis, I retreated to my little room, to swipe on Tinder and sext. Taking dates back to 538 was always a bit of a trip. I have been informed by several partners, lovers and one-night stands that I am non-threatening to a fault, but even my nine-year-old-boy aura only goes so far when you're leading a stranger down a dark alley, onto a quiet street, and into a factory that looks like the lair of an '80s Batman villain. Put it this way: a film once used my street and building to recreate Syria for a film about its civil war.

Still, the place, like me I guess, was so peculiar as to be seductive.

Just about everyone in New York is a transplant of one kind or another, all of them drawn to the city by its myth and promise, and 538 is akin to a living museum piece—a slice of New York that exists solely in people's cultural imagination—a run-down artists loft in the hippest neighbourhood in Brooklyn, filled with genuine desperados, burnouts, and exiles–not the poseur trust fund kids two train stops over in Williamsburg. Places like this simply don't exist in New York anymore; you can list the exceptions on one hand. Indeed, in my time there the real estate collective that owns the property were doing everything to turf the tenants out and turn the place into multi-million-dollar luxury condos (sans glue factory, one imagines). Our landlord—a borderline offensive stereotype of a man who had the ill luck to have the cartoonish name Izzy Israel (I thought my neighbour was being anti-Semitic when he called him this, but no)—and the Russian mafia adjacent businessmen who own 538 had been slightly stymied by their own greed, having rented out the building as a residential property illegally in the first place, and for decades, making it very difficult for them to paint themselves as the good guys in court. So 538 persisted (and persists) as a kinda nowhere place, somewhere tucked between New York fantasy and stark American reality.

But there is nothing like making out on its roof in the summertime, bathed in the pink glow of the giant sun as it sets behind the Manhattan skyline, perfectly framed on our rooftop as if it were a contrived postcard. Despite looking like an interactive guide to hepatitis C, 538 is an incredibly romantic, and seductive, place. One night, a date and I waltzed on the higher roof (there is a four-storey roof higher than my second-storey roof, the building being on a corner and shaped like an L) to the determinedly non-lovey-dovey song 'Spiderman in the Flesh' by the Country Teasers. Our affair lasted a few months, which is close to a five-year marriage in the New York dating scene.

When I first moved into 538, I lived in a coffin-sized room that was, chillingly, painted as a replica of the nightmarish Red Room from David Lynch's *Twin Peaks*—Greek statue and all. Other than being a completely airless nightmare of red-and-black walls and white zigzags, it was an uneasy place to screw people in. 'Ah why yes, this *is* the Red Room from *Twin Peaks*! That's right, the room that represents the repercussive trauma of horrific sexual violence. Fancy some cherry pie?'. Still, it was a claustrophobic hotbox, and something about that, and the various Laura Palmer pictures hanging on the wall, made it a place of frenetic sexual energy, even if it turned my hair bleach-white by the end of my month-long stay within it.

My second room was more of a ship's cabin, notable only for the fact that it sat all but on top of the communal couch, so that any nocturnal activities could be heard by any and everyone in the apartment at the time. To be fair, we could all hear each other's everything all the time, be it sex, crying, bickering or whatever prestige drama we were then bingeing. There wasn't any real privacy, and I was surprised as anyone when that ceased to bother me about a fortnight into my initial stay, as when it comes to sex and romance, I am an incredibly private person (despite what this essay suggests).

My third and final room was upstairs (moving on up!) and where the downstairs rooms were confined, this one was cavernous, and had a defunct factory (fun fact: 538 was originally a doll factory!) piping running through it, which I used to hang my clothes. Of the many people I fucked there, not one didn't have a little swing on the big red mystery pipe, and why not?

A lot of the fun of dating/fucking in New York comes from visiting people's respective spaces. No two apartments (or roommates) are alike, and it's always interesting what gets revealed by the little nests we choose to invite people into. Back home, I have a fastidiously curated bedroom, loomed over by my overflowing library, surrounded by art, and filled out by a large, comfortable, and stylish bed. In New York, I have less control over my hovel (which is just that). I could always clock the moment when a person first took it in and realised that I am that meme of the weird boy without a bed frame come to life—the Bushwick manic-pixie-dropkick.

I found myself curating a growing list of lovers who had incredibly nice places. One girlfriend lived on her own in a one-room apartment on Delancey Street in Manhattan's Lower East Side, a relatively spacious spot with a nice kitchen and bathroom aka a New York miracle. It's a mystery as to how a young student could pay for such a place (until you learn their wealthy parents fork the bill) but it was an oasis from all the bombastic nonsense of my own place, and the city outside. It was an incredibly well-kept and clean little spot in a city where those things had become highly prized rarities. I'd sit there and work during the days when she was at college or working at her gallery and I'd feel my batteries recharge. I think I have a higher tolerance for the more exhausting facets of New York living than most foreign transplants, but even I'd find myself burnt-out or crashing, in desperate need of twenty-four hours of respite from the city's vampirism. The apartments and the beds of others is where I found it for the most part, and I'm thankful that my helpless urchin energy allowed so many people to comfortably leave me unattended in their nice homes, where I merely sat, read, wrote and slept.

Like a lot of autists and OCD folk, I am fairly averse to change. I am a slave to habit and routine, even when I've consciously tried to break free of it. I moved to New York to do just that, as I've said, but after a few years living in the same space I found myself falling into predictable patterns. Wake up, cook brekky, chat guff with Oscar, then amble out and catch the L up to the East Village (where I'd fallen in love with New York as tourist in 2014), to visit the library by Tompkins Square Park, and if hungry, step in for fried chicken at my favourite eatery, Bob White's Supper Counter (which I'd first eaten at on said trip). I'd made that 2014 journey with my then partner, a partner of eventually (almost) five years, who I was deeply in love with—a genius painter as compassionate as they were talented, smart, funny, and beautiful. We'd spent a month on Avenue C in the East Village's Alphabet City, from which we explored New York, with plans of moving there as a couple some distant day in our more settled futures.

Five years later and I still found myself repeating our steps and stopping in at our old haunts, if just to catch a glimpse of my younger self, so sincere in my love yet so cynical in just about everything else. It is strange to leave Perth to flee all the ghosts every street corner holds for you only to plant new ghosts in a city so vast and dense that you trick yourself into believing said ghosts will be lost in the crowd. But they aren't. They're as visible as the Chrysler Building, and you soon find yourself nodding your head at them as you pass by on streets where you've loved, laughed, lost and finger-banged.

I would break myself out of this East Village reverie by walking over to the Lower East Side, and seeing a movie at my favourite cinema, Metrograph. There, I would sink into my chair and watch old film prints of Renoir or Mizoguchi or lost '70s gems like *Wanda* and feel myself refilled with the promise and purpose of New York. Cinema had made me fall in love with this city, and cinema kept that love afloat, even when the film in question had nothing to do with the place itself. New York is a cineaste's city, after all. People pop into places like Metrograph at 2pm on a Tuesday to kneel in prayer and silent observation at the dreams offered up by the projector. It is another escape, another respite, another recharge, for those who have to reconfigure the city back into its romantic and heady fantasia, as opposed to its garish, often banal, reality.

The movies are the place where I first came to truly understand my OCD. Y'see, watching a movie is the only time when I'm behaved: I sit still, I'm respectful, no phone, no talk, and no (NO!) popcorn. I am not an angry person anytime other than when I am in a cinema and someone is making some kind of *noise*. My ex, the painter, used to say it was the only time she ever felt me emanate something close to rage, and almost invariably at the most benign thing: someone chewing, someone scratching themselves, someone opening those *accursed* choc-tops, someone making that 'mmmmhmmm' noise wankers make when they want everyone to know that *they* get it, if *you* don't. The movie houses of New York were the first I'd been to where the other movie goers were as hair-trigger anal as I was about any noise or disturbance. That is to say the movie houses like Metrograph, Film Forum, and IFC. General cinemas in New York (and America) are riotous—it really feels like the *Mad Max* road droogs have slipped in to catch the tail end of whatever Marvel dreck is currently showing, and they're going to hoot and holler and hurl the place down. It's such absolute nuttiness that I kinda end up enjoying it more than the movie itself—yet another example of extremes being more comforting to me than any ill-kept middle ground.

I have only had sex in a cinema once—during a screening of the children's animated feature *The Lorax*—and I still found myself looking at the screen so I could keep track of what's going on.

Credits roll.

## Trouble in Transit

After my ramble and my movie, I'd find myself picking up a fried chicken sandwich at this secret little spot on the fringe of Chinatown whilst setting up the night ahead—maybe drop in at a few comedy mics, see a show, see if my mate Chris wants to hang, or go on a date or head to a hook-up. You never can tell what your night will hold in New York. For even if you find yourself—as I did—falling into a relatively comfortable routine, the city has a way of disrupting it. Particularly if you're depending on the subway to get you from point A to B.

How do you make the MTA laugh? Tell it your plans. The L line, my line, had been damaged by Hurricane Sandy way back in 2012, and the MTA, the mayor, and the governor had spent the better part of the preceding decade kicking the buck between each other, invariably delaying or just plain old mishandling the much-needed repairs. These repairs caused one of the more straightforward Subway lines to become one of the more unpredictable.

A big part of my OCD (and autism) is a strict adherence to timetables. I arrive at everything early, I never miss a deadline, I like to know 'when' whenever people are going on about 'where' and 'what.' Despite being a deeply disorganised person, uncertainty really stresses me out. If the train says it'll arrive at 6.55 and that it'll deposit me where I'm going at 7.35, then by gum it should. This was the sad refrain I and my fellow commuters stranded in the 1st Avenue subway station during a sweltering heat wave would find ourselves repeating as we waited, waited, waited for the crippled L. Before you knew it, you were dumped at Lorimer and prodded onto a replacement bus that spent forty-five minutes going in the wrong direction and making the wrong stops while ignoring the loud (and borderline violent) protestations of its passengers. One such bus took us down a one-way street in a narrow cul-de-sac to the enraged, frothy heckling of all on board (not me, I'd just come back from a lover's in Williamsburg and was dozing off) until it got midway through a thirty-five point U-turn before the driver gave up, unbuckled their seat belt, and wordlessly exited the vehicle to the bemused silence of all on board.

But the subway isn't all bad (for one, it's a great place to read).

At a certain time of day, on a certain type of night, the subway becomes a hotbed of furtive glances and protracted longing. When the fates line up, 1st Avenue to Broadway Junction is a tuna can of young-wired-beautiful freaks, and you find yourself being asked what you're reading, where you're heading, and would you be keen to get a drink. Despite my reputation as a gap-toothed Lothario, I've never approached a stranger at a pub, party or subway stop with the intention of flirting with them—people, women especially, face enough harassment and annoyance without my weird mug prattling on at them about Evel Knievel and such on their way home from work, good *grief*. But my accent drew people to me in New York—the (wrongly imho) exoticised Australian—like moths to a larrikin flame, and offhand chats about quokkas and bilbies soon turned to questions about gun control and giant spider attacks which inevitably led to $3 shots at The Cobra Club which invariably led to some fun, no-strings attached, late evening sex.

New York rewards flexibility. Hold too still, sit too rigid, or stand straight with pride and it will snap you in twain without a second thought. Let go of your rules, your dignity, and your intentions— the city is cold and indifferent to all that, and is doing its darndest to siphon it out of you. Now, that's the kind of thing you'd tell an OCD sufferer if you were trying to describe the deepest bowel of hell, where they were heading for not counting their tissue blows etc. But New York will set you free. You've got to think of it like the most intense exposure therapy out there, cooked up by people who genuinely want you to start having a good time. Lord knows it's about as expensive as therapy, although at least the food is better, and the company is more diverse.

## God's Lonely Man

In Australia, Perth especially, it's easy to feel like the craziest person in the room. Even our lunatics operate with a buttoned-down linearity at the end of the day, landing them an air of predictability. Perhaps I'm the only person that feels this, having spent my entire life living in Fremantle, a place whose most beautiful building is a neo-gothic Germanic asylum. I am quite inured to what some call the 'Fremantle character', worriedly so, because it means I might have become one.

Point is, I am used to seeing people that need a lot of help not receive any.

My friend Hubert, who I met working the bar at Molasses Books in Bushwick in my first week there, once said to me that I had the smoothest street reflexes of anyone he'd ever met:

—You see the crazies coming from a mile off, man. You flow around them like a stream.

Sure, maybe. I don't know. Thirty years of people screaming 'dog cunt' at you while throwing the odd café chair your way will certainly hone your reflexes. It's hard to miss the chronically unwell in Fremantle as they are left to stand like little warning buoys on relatively empty streets. It's harder still to miss the guy jacking off at a postbox when it's just you, him, and a parking inspector strolling down High Street. I'm mad, not blind.

The way Australia treats mental illness is by pretending that it doesn't really exist, while shouting loudly about how *aware* of it we all are. It's a glib little statement but an apt one: people here are much more accepting of mental health than they are of much of mental illness. The genuinely insane get locked up, shipped off, or discarded, and they walk amongst us like the living dead, ignored and overtaken, and never heeded as forewarnings of our own potential trajectories.

I am fairly open about being nuts—heck, I have been exploited by and have exploited Australian media and publishing's ravishing hunger for 'trauma porn' and mental health ~content~ —I am more than aware that our diagnoses is now another identifier to be tacked onto our all-important personal brands, making us easily digestible for the bizarre wonks who toil in the marketing pits of the Australian arts sector, allowing them to better sell us off to the middle-brow journalists they went to private school with two decades prior, who in turn regurgitate ourselves and our work up for the ABCRN crowd. I am invited to contribute to panels, festivals and anthologies because of my diagnoses, where I am requested to perform in a certain way to satiate both the curiosity and the repulsion of both the organisers, managers and audience, who are invariably, themselves, rather uninteresting sorts whose insanity doesn't extend far beyond that of anyone working a nine to five job.

These are the only instances in which madness is permitted to be visible in Australia, and even then, it is collared and leashed and performed on hind legs for last night's scraps. What does one gain by publishing these deeply personal confessionals? Why, far below the minimum wage and a pat on the back from well-meaning strangers who are turning your hurt and illness into product. You can spot the hustle from a mile off and still be suckered by it, such is the way of things.

It does, of course, amount to immense loneliness, both socially and professionally. To be asked to wheel out your infirmities for The Saturday Paper types again and again is already a draining exercise, but to have to do so in a manner that titillates but never terrifies is something else entirely.

Your art suffers for it, of course. Ah, how they *crave* 'neurodivergent' (sounds like something out of *Blade Runner*) 'voices' to publish and champion, but ah! how they flinch away from it when it is put to them honestly, plainly and excitedly. You can't have fun with it. Worse yet! You can't be funny (truly funny, not *Nanette* funny). You can't be funny and mad, nothing drives these people wilder, nothing affronts their bourgeois righteousness more than this. They're here to hear you repent and bemoan, not tell jokes while you talk about being a well-hung cad banging ad execs in the Big Smoke. Tut tut, have mercy on the poor souls, such as yourself etc. It's all exhausting, it's all isolating, and the only way out is through career kamikaze which I have until now only edged.

You're a circus freak, a pitiable cause, a notorious outlaw, and the crowd is baying to hear you speak—which you're permitted to do on the gallows, moments before you're hanged.

Such is the fate of the nutter as artist in Australia, who has been throwing themself into a billabong for a song since time immemorial.

In New York on the other hand, you are rarely the craziest person in the room.

The most high-functioning success stories I've known and befriended in New York would be looked at in Australia as malignant savants with unfixable personality disorders. Like me, these people are obsessives. Like me, these people are *passionate*. Passion, and how we appreciate it, is the thing that sets Australia and America apart.

In the same way Americans love to go on about their freedom while having very little of it, Australians love to go on about how laidback and easygoing we are. A nation of scallywags and ribald scamps, we'd have you believe. Untrue, of course. We were born and will die a nation of middle-class cops whose favourite pastime is tearing people down and cutting them off at the knees. Americans are also a hate-filled lot but their hate is a tumultuous maelstrom of minds, societies, and voices, stitched together in a broken nation state built on one of history's biggest lies and stuffed with all the runner-ups—it is a wild place, and it loves and hates with all the extremeness that wildness affords. Australia, on the other hand, is just Centrelink call-centre mean: dead-eyed, envious, mean-spirited, and unimaginative. Our hate is as bland and consistent as our national cuisine. It doesn't excite us, like America's hate excites them. It just sits in us like a stomach cancer, that we occasionally treat by drinking Mylanta.

I'll say it again for emphasis: Americans are *passionate*.

It's that passion that makes my madness invisible in New York. Americans, New Yorkers *especially*, are an enthusiastic bunch. Despite the city's reputation for being filled with cold-hearted, work-driven nihilists, the opposite is true. New York is a series of small villages strung together like Christmas lights, blinking on and off in kind. You know your neighbours. You know your neighbourhood. You know your community. You can't not: you live on top of each other. To be hateful or prickish is to disrupt the very thing that makes the city work, and you'll soon find yourself cut out, exiled and having a miserable time. In Australia, our suburban sprawl has allowed a country of little kings in little kingdoms to bloom, and rarely if ever do you have to talk with the people two, heck *one,* door over, let alone the guys running the old tyre shop down the block. Our community is reduced to Facebook comment sections, where we let it be known that we hate one another, and it's all your fault.

Americans sincerely *want* to hear about your day, your life, your work, your art, and your *passions.* As an Australian, this took some adjusting to. At one point, there were five Australians (myself included) living in 538. We'd often talk about how when we first moved to New York we felt like people were taking the piss out of us whenever they responded enthusiastically to our interests and passion projects. I know from years of heartbreak and dejection that there's nothing Australians hate more than someone sounding off, obsessively, about what excites them—unless it's cricket (and even then). We are a people who love to undercut one another with assured disinterest, and I found myself reflexively doing so to my American friends, who would look at me as if I'd come into their homes and strangled their cats. I found myself having to apologise not just for me, but for Australia as a whole, and the innate cynicism it imbues you with. It took living and loving in New York to help me unlearn that nastiness, and untrain those reflexes, which I've come to see as national obsessive habits.

It took living and loving in New York for the guilt that had dogged me my whole life for being *too* passionate, *too* obsessive, and *too* imaginative to finally lift.

New Yorkers are verbosely neurotic. They take pride in it. Diagnoses are discussed with the same casual air as where to go for brunch. It's a boring old cliché to say *you don't have to be crazy to live here, but it helps,* but by god, it's difficult to imagine *what* the life of a 'sane' person in New York would even look like.

That is until you go to Times Square.

Times Square, for the easily overstimulated, is a sort of Boschian Hell. As you look up at the billboards for *Wicked*, *Hamilton* and the *SpongeBob* musical and succumb to the siren song of the overtly sexualised green M&M which struts in twenty-foot HD megavision above the M&M store, you can find yourself questioning your grip on this plane of existence.

Surely, you think, this is *insanity*.

But then you look around.

The people enjoying Times Square are not New Yorkers. They're tourists. Many of whom are Australians (I've been this tourist, when I first visited New York with my family as a teenager in 2007). They are also societally 'sane'. These are the middling bulwarks of healthy-mindedness. The mean point by which the rest of us are labelled in contrast of. Here they are, spending $80 to have their photos taken with an illegal immigrant dressed as Batman. Here they are, marvelling at the wax simulacrum of Jimmy Fallon at Madame Tussaud's. Here they are, gazing longingly up at the enticingly leggy gams of the sexy green M&M.

These are the people without obsessions. Without compulsions. Without disorders. These are the people still having sex with their high-school sweethearts. These are the people loudly chewing popcorn in the cinema. These are the people that stand five abreast in the middle of a busy sidewalk to try and find the Empire State Building on a map. These are the people who'd never think of spinning their disabilities, illness or trauma into a naff essay for an audience of strangers. These are the people who read that famous Australian author I can't stand. These are the people who've only ever stolen bank pens, and even then, accidentally. These are the people whose trains always run on time. And Times Square is their kingdom.

On one of my last nights in New York, a family from Sydney's Northern Beaches approached me and asked me if I could take a photo of them in front of all the big advertisements. The husband had a picture of Robert De Niro as Travis Bickle from *Taxi Driver* on his shirt: a shot from the film's penultimate moment, when a bloodied De Niro holds his finger to his head like a gun and mimes shooting himself. It sat oddly next to the pink cheeks of his freckly daughter, who must have been around nine. The other kids were in their early teens. They were all wearing *Wicked* shirts.

I took the photo.

— One more for safety, I said.

Another.

— One more wouldn't hurt.

— I'm sure that's fine.

— Tell you what, let's just make it five so it feels even.

— Ok … sure …

— Five's an odd number but, said the girl.

— Not to me it isn't.

As I walked away, off towards the ACE line, which would take me to the L, which I'd ride to the G, which I'd ride to this beautiful documentarian I'd been seeing, whom I'd ride until we fell asleep, I made sure I stepped over each crack in the sidewalk in a 2-3-2 pattern so that I could swipe onto the subway knowing I'd done my best to dodge the gibbet for one more day, that I'd found some order amongst the chaos, that the gloves I was wearing had retailed at $89.99 in the Guggenheim's gift shop, that I loved New York City—the Kingdom of the Top Root—and that the L train, invariably, would be late.

# Everything Is Cyanide and Nothing Is Safe: Living with Contamination-Based OCD

Dani Leever

*To my fabulous family, to my loved ones,*
*and to pinot grigio*

*Monday 11:17am*
*please don't write 'have a nice day' in the order notes for our online coffee order. what if they think we're being sarcastic and retaliate by pouring bleach into our cups*

*Tuesday 6:29pm*
*i can't leave liquorland because i'm stuck at the back shelf. i'm picking up each merlot and closely analysing the ridges under the cap, checking signs for tampering. i get to the counter, turn back and pick another, because what if the one i chose was poisoned? i imagine a reverse charlie and the chocolate factory competition—instead of a golden ticket, five unlucky winners are killed with cyanide*

When you have OCD, the world moves at a dizzyingly fast pace.

The road bumps that keep me miles behind are everywhere—you'd be surprised how much time adds up when it takes three minutes to walk through a door. To wash and dry my hands to a level that feels comfortable, I may as well put on Taylor Swift's 'All Too Well (10 Minute Version) (Taylor's Version) (From the Vault)'.

Trying to speed up takes energy that you don't always have. When the lion's share of the world feels like it's covered in spikes, you're constantly on high alert. Being on unceasing high alert will make you utterly exhausted.

Although I have a wide variety of symptoms, my OCD is primarily contamination based. Contamination OCD is characterised by a person experiencing intense discomfort when coming into contact with, or being exposed to, something perceived as dangerous, called a 'contaminant'. The person will worry that the exposure to the contaminant will cause them harm, illness or even death. Contamination OCD also can extend to a fear of spreading illness or germs to others and causing *them* harm.

These obsessive thoughts about contamination cause significant anxiety, and can spiral out of control for what feels like an unbearably long period of time. Often, the thoughts ('obsessions') feel like they won't stop until a specific action ('compulsions') is performed in an attempt to 'neutralise' the danger.

A fairly common type of contamination-based OCD involves obsessive thoughts around contracting germs or illness through unclean or unsafe surfaces. This fear can prompt compulsions such as frequent and intense handwashing, avoiding unfamiliar surfaces or objects, excessive cleaning, showering or changing clothes. The compulsion responses that a person with contamination OCD has will vary from person to person, ranging from minorly to majorly disruptive to their everyday life.

Mess has never scared me. I'll happily leave a plate of food scraps in my room if I'm too lazy to move it. I've been consistently criticised at my hospitality jobs for being heinously bad at cleaning tasks. I currently work as a horticulturist, where getting filthy in a garden brings me immense joy—even when I'm faced with squirming bugs, and my arms are elbow-deep in compost.

A common misconception of OCD is that it's simply a matter of just wanting everything to be sparkling clean. But it's more than that. It's the intense dread and paranoid thoughts that come from even being *near* something deemed unsafe. You avoid it like the plague, because it feels like the plague.

A non-exhaustive list of the contaminants that cause me panic on a daily basis: cups, doors, handles, sinks, cutlery, any and all food, liquid of any kind, stickers, hand soap, buttons, plates, bowls, light switches, remotes, furniture, the ground, other people.

*Thursday 9:49am*
*that's the safest mug in the house. it's my favourite because*
*of its big 'wine mum' aesthetic. it says 'before work', and of*
*course kmart provided a wine glass with it that says 'after*
*work'. it's one of the few mugs i can actually use in this house,*
*but i haven't seen it in a week*

*maybe my housemate took it to mix hair dye or paint or drugs*
*or homemade insect repellent in it or something. maybe if i*
*make a coffee in it, the residue of whatever it was will still be*
*there. maybe i'll ingest poison and maybe i'll die on the spot*

I'm twenty-six and I'm sitting in a Pickling 101 class. I'm neither here nor there about pickles, but Angus loves them and he's horrible at making them. In the end, mine turn out better, because I accidentally spilled the entire packet of cumin in my brining liquid.

The instructor asks us all to state our names, what we're hoping to get out of the class and a 'fun fact' about ourselves. A lady named Maryanne goes first. She says she hopes to 'learn how to make pickles, I guess' and tells everyone she's scared of feet.

Her friend Kaz goes next. She says she hopes to 'also learn how to make pickles, I guess', and tells everyone she's scared of mayonnaise.

A lady in the row behind me responds, 'My husband calls me mayonnaise! Because I'm great, but too much of me and I ruin absolutely everything!'

It's the straightest thing I've ever heard. I later learn that the woman's name is Jan, and make a mental note to tell Jan she should immediately divorce her husband.

I'm next. 'Hi, I'm Dani,' I say in my best 'impressing a room of strangers' voice. 'I'm just here because my partner loves pickles. And ... I'm scared of stickers! Seriously—they make me so woozy that I almost throw up,' I say, and I laugh loudly. The room responds with the type of pitying polite laughter you only hear from strangers.

It's my go-to fact, maybe because nobody's ever called me mayonnaise before.

'I'm Angus,' my partner says from next to me. 'I'm hoping to learn how to not make pickles taste like you're drowning in the ocean. My fun fact is one day I came home with tiny dog stickers on each finger as a surprise for Dani, and they ended up having to take a valium.'

*Wednesday 11:17am*
*i can't choose a zucchini in the supermarket because they all look really unsafe*

*this one in the back looks like someone dug their nails into it, and what if they had bleach or something under their nails? the one in front of it looks like a bug has eaten into it, and that could make it really dangerous*

*the one in the very front actually looks fine but it's laughable to think i would ever grab the very front zucchini—the one most people have touched with their hands. i feel dizzy now*

It's hard to think of a time in my life when I didn't exhibit OCD symptoms. The sheer amount of time spent thinking about, and acting on, my obsessions feels embedded into the tapestry of my identity.

I was never a calm child. My mum loves to tell people that I screamed for the first 365 days of my life. Given the person I am now, honestly it checks out.

I started having paranoid thoughts before I was old enough to understand what they even were.

I was diagnosed with depression and anxiety as a teenager. As the only person with a diagnosed mental illness in my immediate family and friendship circle, I always felt like the 'troubled' one. I was seen as dramatic, highly strung and complex—and not just because I'm a Libra.

My OCD symptoms were always there, but none of us knew what they were. I thought it was normal to check under my bed for monsters exactly three times a night before falling asleep. I developed a finger-tapping pattern that I obsessively drummed into my leg hundreds of times a day.

I would have terrifying intrusive thoughts. They'd range from the absurd, suggesting I kick a bird, to utterly horrifying, compelling me to launch myself in front of a train. I would panic at the thought of touching a door handle, and I wouldn't sleep for days because of the hyperrealistic nightmare that my family was about to be murdered.

A key reason why people don't recognise OCD symptoms in themselves or others is the societal misunderstanding of what it actually is.

Many mental illnesses are misused as shorthand for a common experience. 'OCD' is casually used as a synonym for perfectionism. Saying 'I'm so OCD about this' implies you desire something to be a particular way. Some people believe that the worst OCD gets is slight discomfort from seeing a pen out of place.

While craving order and symmetry is a type of OCD, the level of discomfort is severely underestimated. Seeing something out of place, or not being able to order something 'correctly' no matter how many times you try, causes such intense anxiety and distress that you feel like you'll never be able to move on. You can feel as though the earth is off its axis, or even that not being able to correct it will cause you serious harm.

More recently, frequent hand washing has become commonly understood as a key OCD-related behaviour. And although many people with OCD exhibit this behaviour, the distress is, again, underestimated.

If I have an urge to wash my hands and I can't, it feels nothing short of life-threatening.

My catastrophic thinking goes into overdrive, convincing me that I'm in immediate danger. The thoughts are loud and violent. My OCD convinces me that the only way to quell the panic is to wash my hands again and again and again until I get it 'right'.

This also is evident in 'checking' behaviours. Many people will check they've locked the front door as they leave the house, but OCD checking feels like a world of its own. I can stand on my doorstep for fifteen minutes in hysterics, pulling and pushing the locked door over and over again. It's as though there's a signal error—my eyes and hands can believe the door is locked, but my brain just won't listen.

The compulsions (checking, washing, cleaning) are near-impossible to resist. It feels like you're withering away from dehydration—the compulsion then offering itself as a tall glass of ice-cold water.

*Thursday 1:12pm*
*i need to talk to jess right now but they're at work. i don't know if they'll remember but we were eating burritos in bed on sunday and they were on the phone to their mum. i saw a scary thing on the bed like a little mushroom or a little brown thing and they picked it up and put it on the drawers*

*it just fell off the drawers. it's fallen into my clothes on the floor and i can't find it. if it's in my washing then i don't wanna do the washing coz if it's dangerous, it might seep into my clothing. i don't know what to do*

## Concrete slabs and avocado stones

I'm eleven and I've taken forty minutes to walk to the end of my street. I'm needing to get the exact right amount of steps in each slab of concrete on the sidewalk. Some slabs are far smaller than others, so squeezing in the allocated steps takes a lot of concentration.

The very tip of my Converse sneaker touches a crack in the pavement and I start to cry. The spot where the sole of my shoe met the crack feels like it's throbbing. It feels present and painful under my toes. I wonder whether the feeling will ever go away. I picture myself in twenty years, still with an imaginary slice along the bottom of my foot. It feels like it was carved out by piano wire.

I feel wonky. I feel incorrect.

I run back to the top of the street and restart the walk. I slowly and deliberately make my way down, ensuring again that each slab has the same number of steps in it. This time, I make sure that, on alternating feet, I press my toes into the crack of the pavement in the exact spot I originally did.

I desperately try to even myself out. I desperately try to undo the mistake I feel in my body.


It's 2019. My therapist Dr Lucas[1] asks me one hundred questions to determine whether I have OCD. He says he's surprised that no previous therapist had picked up on it.

'Would you say I'm like an OCD poster child?' I ask, grinning. He gives me a slight smirk and carries on with his questions.

'Do you ever have a pervasive uncontrollable thought or fear that your drinks or food have been poisoned?'

I laugh, because the answer is such a resounding yes, that saying the word feels like an understatement. I can't even fathom a life where that fear isn't present. I try to think of the last thing I ate or drank that I didn't assume was poisoned.

'Consider me a yes and fling me into the sun!' I say.

'Do you ever have a pervasive thought or fear that your personal belongings have been tampered with?' he asks.

I look at my water bottle. It's the fourth one I've had this month, because I keep worrying that someone poisoned it while it was lying on the floor of my locked car.

---

1. Not his real name.

'Who told you that?' I say, quoting Alyssa Edwards from *RuPaul's Drag Race All Stars*. Feeling the need to constantly make my therapist laugh is something I'm unpacking in therapy.

He laughs and scribbles on his notepad. Before our very last session together, he does confirm that he thinks I'm funny—thank God.

'Okay, have you got any fears or discomfort around sticky substances? Like stickers or glue?'

I think back to my Pickling 101 workshop. My whole sticker bit is not such a fun fact anymore.

At least I'm not mayonnaise.

*Tuesday 8:50am*
*i wonder what it would be like to walk up to a cupboard, pick any random plate and just use it. that is an utterly bizarre concept*

*the number of safe mugs is dwindling in my own house again*

Having OCD has made me extraordinarily good at thinking on the spot. I often have just seconds to come up with a reason why I will or won't do something, so my brain is always seeking for something that will be perceived with normalcy.

My 'OCD excuses' can sometimes make me laugh. They're wacky, and I often surprise myself with how creative they can get.

I live by these OCD excuses, because the stigma and misconception of my illness is so pervasive. I often wonder what relief and ease would come from a wider comprehensive understanding of what obsessive compulsive disorder really entails. If the image that came to mind for the general population wasn't a Rubik's cube with a single misplaced colour. Or a row of pencils, with one slightly shorter than the rest. Of course, those can cause severe panic in some, but the experience of OCD is often far more complex than media representation will have us believe.

At a party one night, a person asked to have a drag of my cigarette. Knowing that sharing germs with a total stranger was off the cards, I offered to give them the rest of the cigarette.

'I've been meaning to quit actually,' I told them. 'Here, have the rest of it, don't worry about giving it back!'

I somehow convinced them that at that *very moment*, I had quit smoking. And they bought it.

For the rest of the night, I smoked in the very corners of the party, hoping not to be sprung by them. I felt like a naughty teenager hiding their habit from a parent—standing with a friend behind a tree, scrambling and cackling with laughter if we saw the person coming toward us.

I was once offered a slice of pecan pie by a work friend. As a safety precaution, I asked for a list of the ingredients. After being met with a confused look, I blurted out, 'It's so I can see if I've used the same recipe.' I've never made pecan pie.

I was given a list of ingredients that had my OCD alarm bells ringing (sugar from my neighbour, found this vanilla essence at the very back of the cupboard, pecans from my brother's friend). My first thought was to claim a rare vanilla essence intolerance. Of course, there were follow-up questions, which I somehow got through unscathed. Maybe that one term of improv class in high school drama really sunk in.

There are friends in my life who love to laugh with me about my OCD excuses. I talk to them about the utter shenanigans I get myself into, and we can't help but cackle at them. Sometimes I have to double down on something that is complete and utter bullshit.

Once when offered homemade cookies by a housemate's friend, I asked them where they had bought their flour and sugar from. Being able to discuss the process of something being made and where it came from can sometimes bring me comfort.

'Coles. How come?' they replied.

'Oh, because today there was a special at Woolworths on plain flour. I just bought some and it was cool. Was going to see if we could bond over that.'

I walked out of the room with a puzzled expression. What the fuck had I just said?

My ad-libbing skills come to me as a surprise. In general, I'm hideously honest and truly can't keep a secret to save my life. I have told myself strictly to never use this skill for evil or deliberate deception.

I really wish that saying 'I have OCD' didn't lead to invasive follow-up questions, strange looks or laughter. I've tried saying that in the past, but am often immediately reminded why it's not a good idea.

I once had a housemate who despised me for my OCD. She'd openly mock my symptoms, and yell at me every time I double-checked the door. I get it—the sound was pretty annoying inside the house. But she asked me to stop like it was a switch I could simply turn off. When I explained to her how difficult it was, she told me I was delusional. That I wasn't trying hard enough.

I saw her at a bar months after she'd moved out. I used hand sanitiser during our conversation.

'You must think I'm just fucking disgusting and filthy, hey,' she sneered.

Once, I told a waiter that I'd love a new fork after mine fell on the ground. 'I have OCD, so a new fork would be great if possible.'

'I'll make sure to place it evenly on the table then,' he replied, laughing loudly.

Once, I declined a cup of coffee from a colleague, citing OCD as the reason.

'What the fuck does OCD have to do with coffee? Or wait, do you think I'm trying to poison you?' she replied.

Once, I asked a housemate not to use my favourite cup to mix his acrylic paints. 'I have OCD, so I really would love it if my cups were only used for drinking liquids,' I said.

'It's a free country,' he replied.

My OCD fibs are elaborate, often burning up endless creative juices. I hate lying, and even more so, flexing a muscle that allows me to do so.

But the stigma is real, and it's pervasive. I'd rather try to ad-lib an excuse than walk into a debate about the very existence of the illness that crushes me on a daily basis.

*Monday 1:40pm*
*i'm on google and i'm trying to figure out why my avocado has these little lumps on the inside. maybe the lumps in the avocado are from a poisonous pesticide. some of my search results are saying they're a natural reaction to the bumps in the flesh*

*but now i'm on a pdf called 'avocado fruit quality problem solver' by a company called hort innovation. page 2 and 4 are aesthetic shots of beautiful pristine avocados and i don't know if it's supposed to be helpful in my panicked state. page 6 is a closeup of a hand holding an avocado, and i just wish they would get to the point already. i get to page 27 before i realise it's a guide for those growing avocados. i'm sitting here holding something i'm scared is going to kill me*

*a facebook page has told me maybe it's from 'a fruit spotting bug from the rainforest' and now i want to die*

*i'm on a daily mail article called 'holy guacamole! shopper is left baffled by mystery lumps in her avocado—but there is a simple explanation'. the simple explanation is the specific fruit spotting bug bites. avocados australia says the avocados themselves are still safe to eat but what has the heinous daily mail literally ever done for me in the work bathroom, i call jess and cry before i throw the avocado out*

*my avocado panic has taken me to a reddit page called 'what is this thing'. a person, who may or may not be the baffled shopper, has uploaded pictures of a very lumpy avocado. the comments are convinced it's bug bites. i'm glad i threw it out*

*now i'm calming myself down in this subreddit, reading people debate what the 'weird sloped thing in my airbnb's hot tub' is*

*nobody knows, but a battle has started out about how frogs and toads, according to one redditor, are the 'primary accidental-drowning-victims of hot tubs'. the more you know*

*apparently people on google have also searched for*
*– is it okay to eat stringy avocados*
*– is it safe to eat avocado with worms*
*– what happens if you eat bad avocado*
*– why is my avocado hard and rubbery*
*– are avocados a fruit*
*– are avocados vegan*

When I received an OCD diagnosis, it honestly put so much of my life into perspective. I looked back on so many habits, thoughts and 'quirks' that I'd exhibited throughout my life, and now I had a new understanding of them. I can imagine that this isn't an uncommon experience.

Receiving a diagnosis for any mental illness can be daunting and illuminating all at once. You can feel terrified—like you're standing at the bottom of the steepest hill. You're staring up at what's about to be a long and arduous journey of healing, learning and coping. You're steeling yourself to experience stigma, whether it's from others or from yourself.

But you can also feel sheer relief. It can feel like a mystery has been lovingly solved. Like all of the terrifying things you experience actually do have a name, an explanation. Your understanding of your experience deepens. Despite what your illness tells you, you're not the only person on earth to experience this. You're not beyond help.

What I found most shocking about my diagnosis was how I hadn't seen any of the ostentatious flashing neon signs earlier. I've worked in health advocacy for years, and because of that, I would say I have a reasonably high literacy around mental illness.

But even I couldn't understand what was happening. The hours I'd spend washing and rewashing cups, or convincing myself a light switch was covered in poison—these were actually *explainable symptoms*. Before my diagnosis, I thought I was beyond fixing.

Utter relief hit me, as I started to see how my seemingly mystery symptoms weren't all that unusual. So terrifying parts of my life could neatly fit into a diagnosis—it was nothing short of mind-blowing.

*Monday 10:34pm*
*if people with unclean hands touch the top of a hand sanitiser pump, does that mean the pump is contaminated? or is it that the germs get killed straight away, so it doesn't matter? i can't decide what feels safer—exposing myself to germs only to kill them immediately? or not sanitising at all*

I'm thirteen and I'm sitting at a baseball game in New York City. My diehard-Yankee-fan dad has taken me to see his team play the Mets. Auntie Lorraine has bought me and my sister a Mets hat—it's caused quite the family stir.

Despite our lounge-room TV playing a constant stream of baseball at home, I haven't got a single clue how the game works. The entirety of my knowledge of baseball starts and ends with *Twilight*.

All I can think about is the Cullens, speeding around in their embarrassingly matching get-ups and ill-fitting baseball caps to Muse's garish hit 'Supermassive Black Hole'. They're using superspeed and fanciful vampire instincts to host an entirely rigged game, that they somehow expect human Bella to umpire. Kristen Stewart, get *out* of there.

My daydreaming is interrupted by spotting something strange. I zero in on the giant screen telling us the score. I see the fixtures holding it up, and one looks to be missing a gigantic bolt. Seven other bolts are in place, but the missing one is burning in my eyes.

I try to picture the trajectory of where it would fall. I extrapolate that me and my whole extended family is about to be obliterated. The section where we are sitting in the stadium is moments away from being reduced to rubble.

I point the missing bolt out to an uncle between panicked breathing.

'It's probably nothing,' he says, keeping his eyes on the match happening. Hideki Matsui is about to take the plate, and the crowd is going wild. He's one of the few players I recognise; he's a family favourite.

I'm speechless at how he can be so blasé about something so ominous and out of the ordinary. Forgetting about the bolt is not an option. I spend the entirety of the game with my head between my knees.

*Sunday 11:49pm*
*i don't know how to ask the bartender for a glass of water. he*
*keeps pointing to the communal jug, but i'd sooner rip out my*
*own teeth before drinking out of communal water at a bar*

*'i'd really rather my own glass if that's okay,' i say*

*'what's wrong with you? nobody's going to waste their precious drugs just trying to fuck with a bunch of strangers, if that's what this is about' he says, free-pouring a shot of whisky for the guy next to me*

## The farm party

Like many mental illnesses, the mechanics of how someone develops OCD are highly individualised and complex. Despite what my Google search history may indicate, I'm no expert.

When I look back on my growing up, I can see the beginnings of what would eventually become a diagnosis. The counting of steps along the sidewalk, the paranoia around surfaces and germs and the obsessive thoughts were all weaving a tapestry of OCD.

But in the space of poison and how it seeps into my food and drink, one night sits heavily inside my bones. It kicked off a terrifying trajectory that saw me get more and more unwell.

In 2015, I had a very bad year. I was working a job I hated, was in the process of losing most of my friends as I was coming out as queer, and I was in a toxic relationship that would scar the inside of my brain forever.

For my birthday, Bradley[2] wanted to go to his friend's giant farm party. I wasn't particularly keen on the idea, but was particularly keen on keeping him happy, so we went.

During the car trip up, I told him I was feeling a little anxious as I wouldn't know anyone, and famously wasn't the greatest at camping.

'I'm going to this festival to expand my mind, and it's up to you whether you join me on that journey,' he replied nonchalantly.

As soon as we parked the car, I held my head in my hands and started to quiver. I was anxious as all hell being in the middle of nowhere with none of my creature comforts. A part of me knew

---

2. Not his real name.

then how much I despised the space and how out of place I was. But we were there for Bradley, so I forced myself to pull it together.

We walked around and took in the scenery—a guy passed out with sunnies in a camp chair, ciggy butts and nang canisters covering the ground, and a pair of boys with bucket hats fighting over who would go next on the DJ decks that were sitting atop milk crates. My nails dug into my palms. I tried so hard to play relaxed, to seem 'chill' and 'easygoing'—two things I proudly can admit now that I am not.

Over the distorted sound of psytrance and techno blasting through cheap speakers, every few minutes you'd hear a loud shout. It was the kind of grunting shout that signalled winning a drinking game, or just the loud noise of loud boys asserting their loudness.

'Nothing bad can happen to me here,' I told myself, trying to believe that the loose vibe of the party translated into tangible safety.

At one part of the farm, there was a makeshift Old Western–style tavern. It seemed out of place from the rest of the party—more camp and polished than the other dingy corners of the farm. Behind the constructed wooden bar were three people dressed as cowboys. They flung whisky into the shot glasses of eager patrons and yee-hawed in unison at every chance they got. The space was lively and exuberant—everyone was having a great time.

A few uneasy hours later, I became separated from Bradley and looked for him at the tavern. I'd had a single glass of cheap wine in a vain attempt to quell my anxiety. I desperately looked around, when a man behind the bar called out to me. He wasn't in a cowboy get-up, which was strange. He asked me if I wanted a drink.

'Oh! You're part of the cowboy bar? Okay sure,' I said. 'Do you have any of that whisky from before?'

'I don't, but I do have this Carlton Draught,' he replied, pulling an open can out from under the bar.

I took the drink and had a sip. It was from behind a bar that many people were sitting at, and the space still felt as energetic and lively as it had before.

The man came around from the other side of the bar and asked me if I wanted to sit somewhere more private. 'I love your energy,' he told me.

'Oh, no thanks. I should probably go look for my boyfriend,' I said. It was a line I'd used all too frequently to get out of situations that were feeling strange.

'That's fine, he'll come find you soon! My girlfriend's around somewhere too,' he replied. He didn't seem too menacing, but I could feel myself tensing up.

Suddenly, I saw the back of Bradley's head and sprung up from my stool.

'Thanks for the drink,' I called out as I ran off.

The next thing I remember, it was 12pm the next day.


*Wednesday, 11:18am*
*i know that used to be my favourite mug, but i think my old housemates hated me so much they put drugs into it to freak me out*


I woke up in a panic, feeling like I'd been hit by a bus. I shook Bradley's friend awake and asked her what happened.

'Oh, you were acting super weird and fucked, so we put you to bed at like ten thirty,' she said sleepily.

I desperately scrambled for a sense of perception to explain what had happened. From the second I had a drink from the tavern, my memory felt like a television with a scrambled connection.

Head pounding, I bolted out of the car and ran around the farm, looking for Bradley. I found him in a corner, drinking a warm beer in a deck chair. He barely looked up.

'Babe, I really need you. I can't figure out what's happened and I think my drink was spiked,' I told him.

He told me it was probably bullshit.

'Who spikes drinks these days,' he muttered between drags on a half-lit cigarette.

I explained that I'd missed the whole night and only had one solid memory before completely blacking out.

'Luckily Rebecca[3] was there, apparently she put me to bed,' I said, which didn't garner a response from him.

On the car ride home, he told me he was glad we'd spent the night apart. He'd taken a ton of acid and was worried I was going to 'annoy' him.

*Tuesday 4:40am*
*did that dinner i cooked look a bit weird? Was that blue streak from the cabbage or did something dangerous fall in?*

*I'm on google and the reason that red cabbage turns blue has something to do with acidity, alkaline and pH levels. apparently adding lemon juice will turn a blue cabbage back to red. i've already eaten the blue cabbage so it's too late to add lemon juice. maybe without the lemon juice the cabbage is toxic, and maybe I won't wake up in the morning and i didn't even say goodbye to anyone*

## Just call me 'Elbows'

The night of my diagnosis, despite my therapist's strict instructions not to get carried away on the internet, I end up becoming enthralled with a fictional woman called Sandra. Fictional Sandra has severe contamination-based OCD.[4]

Fictional Sandra is in a shopping centre and needs to use the bathroom. She panics; fears of germs and illness flood her mind. Attempting to reduce her anxiety and prevent any possible contamination, Sandra avoids touching absolutely everything in

---

3. Not her real name.

4. treatmyocd.com/blog/contamination-ocd-fear-of-germs

the bathroom—the door, toilet, sink, light switch.

'After using the bathroom, she washes her hands aggressively for several minutes until she "feels clean,"' the example states.

'Despite the thorough wash, Sandra struggles to cope with the uncertainty that her hands may remain contaminated. She returns to the sink and washes once more, this time up to her elbows. Upon leaving the restroom she still feels uncertain that her hands are completely clean,' it continues.

'In order to relieve the doubt, Sandra ends up washing and sanitizing periodically for the next hour. Her hands appear chapped and sore, and a quick shopping trip has turned into a long ordeal.'

Looking down at my dried-up cracked hands on the keyboard, it appears as though Fictional Sandra and I have had a very similar day.

I think about the hours of my life I've spent gingerly laying down paper towels on a toilet seat, or burning my thigh muscles to hover and avoid contact altogether. I think about the countless sinks that I've operated with my elbows, and the sheer gratitude I've felt for whoever designed the entirely contactless systems you'll sometimes see at airports.

My elbows have often been the fall guy for my hands, interacting with whatever looks the most poisonous. Often, after particularly spiky public bathroom trips, my elbows feel hot. I become hyper-aware of the specific section of skin that's made contact with something dangerous. Every ounce of attention I have in my body rushes toward it.

The spot feels like it's burning a hole in my skin. It pulsates, and I'm so focused on it that my vision goes blurry. Minutes pass, and all I can think of is how the germs are swarming and multiplying like tiny bugs. Any second now, the bugs will race and crawl up my arm and around my body, and I will die. The thoughts don't stop until I rub hand sanitiser on my elbow.

I wonder if Fictional Sandra has ever rubbed hand sanitiser on her elbow so hard that it bled at Northland Shopping Centre.

*Friday 12:45pm*
*i touched the myki reader with the corner of my finger when*
*i was touching on. i don't have hand sanitiser and i think*
*maybe i'm going to die*

*Saturday 11:18am*
*i'm so upset because chemist warehouse is sold out of the only*
*coconut hand cream that works on my fucking dry chapped*
*hands. it brings me so much joy, that hand cream. the scent*
*evokes feelings of self kindness and forgiveness for all the shit*
*i put my body through*

I've always been careful with my drinks. It was drilled into me early on to always keep an eye on your drinks, particularly at a bar or a club.

I'd had one drink-spiking experience before the farm party. I was at a bar in Fitzroy, and a guy was hanging around a little too close to me. I'd had two wines, but noticed my body began slowing down at an alarming rate. I crawled outside and into a cab. I had no idea what was happening, but my body said 'Run'.

When I passed out almost immediately, the cab driver took my phone, searched for 'Mum' in my contacts and called her. Thanks to him, my inability to set a passcode, and my mum's extremely light sleeping, I was home safe in bed before anything worse could happen.

After the farm party, I noticed that I watched my drinks a little closer. A little turned to a *lot* closer, and soon, a lot closer became *obsessively* close. I wouldn't take my eyes off my drink, even in a tucked-away bar booth with someone I loved. I'd refuse any drinks being brought to me—the sheer panic that a bartender or passerby had maybe snuck something into the glass would turn every vein in my body cold.

It wasn't long before drinks in bars became drinks in cafés, and eventually drinks at home. Home alone, I'd pour a glass of water and leave it in the kitchen. I'd go brush my teeth and return to the glass. I would stare at it—lifeless and clear—and convince myself that somebody had broken into my house as I brushed my teeth. They hadn't stolen anything, they were merely there to put poison into my water.

The paranoia only became more intense over time.

I would be watching a drink obsessively, but convince myself that my eyes had missed something. That the moment I blinked was when someone spiked it.

It got to a point where all food and drink, whether it's from my house, the supermarket or a friend, is unsafe and poisonous until proven otherwise. Although I've come a long way in managing this immense fear, it's still extraordinarily distressing.

*Monday 8:21pm*
*i didn't even think it was possible for my hands to be so wet.*
*i've been rinsing the same mug over and over and over again*
*in my kitchen sink. i can't seem to get it right. i remember*
*buying this mug; it's always been safe. but how do i know it's*
*still safe? will water neutralise every part of the danger?*

I'm fifteen and I'm standing in the bathroom of my high school. I'm packing on foundation like my life depends on it. I'm combing a Maybelline Great Lash mascara wand through my dry eyelashes. A pair of year sevens come in and ask me if I'm going to a party after school.

I say no, hopping on a soapbox to declare that makeup is good for any time and any occasion. But really, I'm getting coffee in Hawthorn with a girl, and I haven't figured out if she, too, thinks it's a date. She likes My Chemical Romance, so I flick my eyeliner extra sharp.

The year sevens giggle at me as they run out, mumbling to

each other about how wearing visible makeup is against the school rules.

I see the door swing closed behind them. I stare at the door handle. Just this month, I've started noticing these new weird fears around germs. My brain becomes loud and angry. I push the thoughts down but, like trying to push a beach ball beneath a wave, they fight back. Hard.

It's the first time I ever panic that I potentially won't be able to leave a room.

I try listening to the thoughts, to understand what about the door handle exactly is making me feel unsafe. But all I hear is a violent noise in my ear telling me that touching it will cause me immeasurable pain. I awkwardly manoeuvre the door with my elbows and my T-bar shoes, taking several minutes to pry myself out.

A few classmates catch the act from outside the toilet block. I immediately get the nickname 'Elbows'.

## 'Murder on the Dancefloor (Exposure Therapy Remix)'

*Wednesday 8:46pm*
*i can't get out of the car, i'm completely stuck. i've tried getting out, but i just can't accept the fact that the handbrake is definitely on. i can see it with my eyes, i can touch it with my hand, but my brain just can't receive the message that it's safe. when i try to get out of the car, all i can think about is it rolling and smashing into the van parked in front of me. i don't understand how my eyes and my brain are perceiving the same information completely differently. how do i get out of this car?*

After I got my OCD diagnosis, so much of my life completely changed. I had a lens that I could apply to my 'confusing' actions, scary thoughts and obsessively repeated habits. I decided to write down in my Notes app every time I noticed an OCD moment—an intrusive thought, a moment that harmed me, an assurance-seeking message I sent or even a time I managed to work through a symptom.

Writing these things down became an empowering, albeit terrifying, experience. OCD has the odd power to convince you that your intrusive or obsessive thoughts are borne from your deliberate self. They're representative of the entirety of you and how you feel—they *are* you. As I began writing my obsessions down, I started to see how untrue, absurd and rooted in paranoia so many of them were.

They were far less scary if I looked them directly in the face. It felt like I was a kid, scared of the shadows ominously dancing on the wall, and somebody had turned on the lights.

They were no longer omnipresent thoughts hiding out, directing me like a puppet. They were typed words on a page. I felt power over them.

Facing them directly also allowed me to see how destructive they were. I felt shame reading them, like their existence reminded me of my brokenness. But I was becoming armed with knowledge—about the illness, about myself and what healing looked like. This made confronting and fighting them far easier.

I was developing language for what was happening to me. 'There's an obsession,' 'that's just an intrusive thought,' 'paranoia striking again right there,' I would tell myself.

'Jesus, that one's bloody new,' I would respond to a particularly creative intrusive thought. Engaging with them in this way felt like evening the playing field.

Dread was slowly melting away. I was taking control.


*Tuesday 7:10pm*
*i'm okay with the salt shaker, because it looks safe. but that pepper cracker was just bought from an op shop, so there's*

*absolutely no chance i could use it. i can't track its history, so how can i track whether it's been safe?*

When I first heard about what exposure and response prevention therapy entailed, I thought my life was over.

Dr Lucas told me how it's an effective method of working through OCD, and that we'd be managing it closely together.

The idea is that exposing a person to their greatest fear, over time and in controlled environments, will reduce the panic associated with that fear. So much of phobia is rooted in thoughts that, however irrational they may actually be, feel like scripture.

Exposure therapy relies on a human process called 'habituation'. Habituation occurs when a person is repeatedly exposed to a certain stimulus—an object, place, thought or fear. Habituation occurring means that the brain's response to that stimulus decreases significantly over time.

Think of a person with a phobia of flying (relatable). Putting them on a plane straight away would feel like torture. But slowly exposing them to plane-related stimuli (watching flights on TV, visiting an airport, watching planes take off) over time, the fear response should markedly lessen. Eventually, the treatment suggests, the person's fear will be diminished, potentially to the point of eradication.

For OCD, exposure therapy operates by challenging a person to let obsessive thoughts occur without attempting to 'neutralise' them with compulsions. For example, a person may perceive that their hands are unclean. The obsessions can get louder and louder, urging the person to perform the compulsion of washing or sanitising their hands.

Compulsions feel as though they're immediately eliminating the danger, but in the long run, they push you into avoidance. They become almost addictive, as though harm could come to you if you don't act on them.

In a controlled environment, exposure therapy for OCD means letting the obsessions run wild, without the person acting on the compulsion. Over time, the thoughts quieten down, and the person can see that they're not in any danger. As no tangible negative consequences occur, the person's fear should eventually start to disappear.

When my therapist outlined this to me, a wave of dread washed over me. As if the key to healing my OCD would be to force me into the most terrifying situations imaginable?! Can't there be a simple spell Dr Lucas can put on me to cure the ills of this?

That night, I'm again disappointing Dr Lucas by getting stuck in OCD Google. I'm searching about OCD exposure therapy and see a stock image of a man licking the bottom of a shoe. His expression is titillated and aroused, and I wonder how this image has travelled so far from the shoe-fetish web to the 'I'm terrified and Googling my OCD symptoms' web.

Google tells me that other people have searched for 'can a person with OCD live a normal life?' Curious as to my very fate, I click into it.

I see a deeply heterosexual image of a woman with an extremely large scarf staring lovingly into the eyes of her stock-image-looking male partner.

'If you have OCD, you can undoubtedly live a normal and productive life. Like many long-term illnesses, managing your OCD requires a focus on day-to-day coping rather than on an ultimate cure,' the website assures me.

I wonder if I should be looking forward to a life of extremely large scarves and heterosexuality.

*Friday 12:45pm*
*i'm halfway to the tram stop but did i lock the door? I know i did, because i stood there for ten minutes pulling at the locked handle. my mind is infested with the thought of it swinging open in the spring breeze and i'm running back again and again and again and again*

I'm twenty-seven and I'm wearing the skimpiest outfit you can imagine backstage at a gay club. I've just finished a DJ set and I'm grateful that I'm at a club but in a safe spot. I often wonder if the reason I became a DJ was so that I could go to a scary place like a bar or a club, but have some level of control over the night.

I've put my belongings down, and I'm excited to emerge into the main room of the club and see my partner. While I was DJing, the smile on Jess's face was priceless. They were bursting with pride, even if they'd never be caught dead in a glittery club like this.

The loose sleeves of a hoodie, which I usually rely on to open a door handle, are not currently at my disposal. I'm wearing a one-piece lycra swimsuit and hot pants, so I couldn't pull the material far enough out to cover a door handle even if I wanted to.

I think of the germs on the door handle and how they hold the secrets to my immediate death. I've had a couple of vodkas, so I'm even more incapable than usual of talking myself out of this paranoia.

My hands are tucked into the back of my hot pants, unable to move.

I stand at the door for three minutes and fifty seconds. It's the exact time it takes for the DJ on the other side of the door to play 'Murder on the Dancefloor' by Sophie Ellis-Bextor. It's my favourite song. I love it so much that I almost forget what's happening.

The sound suddenly becomes muffled as someone backstage closes a window to the stage. Losing the song snaps me back into reality.

I can almost see the germs swarming around the door handle. They appear to writhe and contort around the metal bend. The hundreds of people in the venue make the situation feel unbearably claustrophobic. How many people have touched the handle and how could I possibly know what they've all touched beforehand?

All I want is to burst through the door and see Jess, but this door feels like my final boss in a video game. My brain plays out elaborate threatening scenarios. For what feels like forever, I am frozen.

What if the last person who touched the door handle was on their way to roofie someone? If I touch it, the residue will seep into my skin. Then, later on, I will touch my mouth and pass out. I will hit my head on the speaker next to me on the way down.

Finally, a performer from the night emerges from the green room. They have winged eyeliner out to their ears and a shiny black bob. They have on thick black combat boots with a cacophony of chains and buckles wrapped around them.

I sheepishly ask if they'll open the door for me. They greet me with a warm smile, and without a single follow-up question, they theatrically open the door wide for me. I duck under their arm and say thank you as I escape onto the dancefloor.

A DJ later that night plays 'Murder on the Dancefloor' again, and it feels like a victory anthem put on just for me.

I often wonder if that performer ever understood how they saved my life on the night that Elbows couldn't.


*Monday 7:07pm*
*i'm standing in front of the fridge, staring at the cheese block on my shelf. i could have sworn i bought bega brand cheese but this isn't bega brand cheese. perhaps what has happened is that someone has eaten my cheese and replaced it with something dangerous that's going to kill me? my brain is going haywire and why won't it shut up?*

*i just sat down away from the fridge for twenty minutes. my desire for cheese on this pasta has somehow outweighed the power of these fucked-up thoughts. i feel grateful for how much i love cheese right now, because i ate it and even though it was terrifying, i didn't actually die*

## Safety Boy

I'm sixteen and I've made a decision that I can no longer go to large concert halls or music venues. Particularly the ones with gigantic chandeliers.

I see a comedy show at the Forum and can't take my eyes off the roof. I fixate on the flimsy-looking chains holding up enormous light rigs and count the individual shards of glass that would pierce my face if the chandelier crashed down onto us.

When I think of the missing bolt at the baseball stadium, the steps on the sidewalk, the bathroom door handle or the chandelier at the Forum, all I can think of is how relentless my mind has always been. It's like a treble hook, mercilessly latching itself to a thought and refusing to let up.

My mind becomes enamoured with the idea of panic—that a missing bolt could kill me, that the roof will cave in, that my stove is still on, that a surface is dirty, that my food is poisoned. Ever since I was a child, fighting's seemed futile.


It's near impossible for OCD not to seep into the close relationships in your life.

The longest relationships I've had have been a huge part of my OCD healing process. When the world seems terrifying at every turn, all you search for is safety. Sometimes that comes in the form of comfort and care from a person you love.

My brain moves at a million miles an hour, convincing me of every horrid worst-case scenario. So seeking validation or reassurance is a normal instinct. I developed shorthand with my partner Jess, who could quell any of my anxieties with just a word, or a reassuring touch. They know my OCD like they know the lyrics of their favourite Camp Cope song, often moving into comfort mode as soon as they see one of my OCD triggers.

They're often complicit in my exaggerated OCD fibs—jumping in to make an excuse for why I need a new glass of water, or why I simply won't try their housemate's mystery cheesecake. They can sense danger from a mile away, and help me move through it.

Jess's nickname becomes 'Safety Boy'. In a way, it feels like they're the line of defence between me and the scary parts of the world.

We laugh for hours about the unhinged things they do to comfort me or prove that something's safe. It may be eating a slice of an unfamiliar cheese, or it could be straight up drinking rice wine vinegar. They've cracked pepper directly into their mouth, eaten a spoonful of vegemite, sipped on fish sauce and eaten raw onion for me. They keep my side table stocked with my favourite coconut hand cream—the one that makes me feel soothed. Safety Boy takes their job very seriously.

My therapist rightly pointed out that seeking external assurance or validation can become an obsession in itself. Your brain frantically drowning in fear will latch onto a sense of safety if it sees one. Instead of fighting your own terrifying thoughts, you turn to an outsider's sense of assurance.

You search for someone or something that can give you the definitive validation—you're not in danger. After all, somebody else's reassuring words can feel more concrete than your anxious brain. But once you do this enough, dealing without it seems daunting.

What can I do while Jess is at work, but I need someone to tell me the mushrooms I bought from the supermarket are perfectly safe? Am I actually strong enough to give myself the validation?

I know that assurance-seeking is something I deeply need to wean off. So Safety Boy sits with me while I process my fears and obsessive thoughts. As I try to challenge myself not to use them as a validation method, we practise sitting together softly, and I allow myself to move through the discomfort of being exposed to a contaminant. They stroke my hair or give me soft 'scritchies' along my arm. They cuddle me close and kiss my forehead. Because they know that always, always helps.

I had an old friend that I'd often travel interstate with for work. He was my shield to the terrifying unknowns of life on the road—

opening doors, holding my hand on turbulent flights and easing my nerves if an OCD flare-up was happening.

I once tried to explain what living with OCD was like to him. We walked into a breakfast buffet and I stretched my arms out.

'Everything looks like cyanide here,' I sang to a brilliant made-up tune. 'I'd first stick a needle into my eyeball before trying any of that pre-poured coffee left unattended at the table.'

He laughed at the song, but not at its content. He pulled me in for a cuddle. 'Come here, buddy, I gotcha,' he said. His hugs always did make things better.

I mentioned to him on one work trip that my therapist was encouraging me to stop asking for external validation. That it was creating a pattern of *needing* assurance externally, which was a compulsion in itself.

'So I'm just supposed to shut you down when you're in panic mode? What about if everything looks like cyanide and you're crying?' he asked.

It was a fair point. It's a tough thing to break out of. How do you stop someone's caring validation from being the only thing helping you not fall apart?

*Saturday 4:37pm*
*hey, our airbnb hosts aren't going to murder us in the middle of the night are they*

*Saturday 4:39pm*
*their rating was really good and i feel like if they were murderers a previous guest would have figured it out*

*Tuesday 5:20pm*
*i just brought my groceries in without scrubbing the outside obsessively. listing this under ocd wins for sure. dr lucas will be so proud*

The first exposure therapy activity I tried was grabbing a mug from the therapy clinic's communal kitchen and—without *rinsing* it out—drinking water. I'd rather turn up to work and realise I'm completely naked.

Dr Lucas waited for me to return with the cup, and I slowly brought it to my mouth. He observed me with his pen at the ready.

I drank a few gulps of water and my body flashed from hot to cold.

Leaning forward eagerly, Dr Lucas asked how I was feeling. 'Tell me the thoughts you're having right now.'

'I'm absolutely about to die,' I mumbled just loud enough for him to hear.

We sat in silence—the only sound filling the air was the scratching of his pen on paper.

Each heartbeat felt like proof that I was going into cardiac arrest. I felt the anxiety in my body spike for minutes.

And then ... nothing.

After six or seven minutes, my heart rate finally began to lower, and the burning pulses beneath my skin subsided almost entirely.

Dr Lucas kept scribbling on his piece of paper. I was expecting an 'I told you so' grin, but all I saw was compassion. I was safe.

*Sunday 7:44pm*
*i just ate completely random pumpkin pie at an event. a*
*whole baked pumpkin pie at a staff event, and i just ate it.*
*i was scared out of my mind but it was totally fine. that's a*
*huge step. who is this new dani, seriously?*

I'm watching *Work in Progress* with my partner. The semi-autobiographical character Abby (played by Abby McEnany) has a meltdown in a public bathroom that lasts most of the episode.

Abby is a butch lesbian. The scene revolves around how bathrooms trigger a serious OCD panic, as well as unwarranted comments around Abby's gender presentation and perceived gender.

Abby washes her hands over and over again, starting and restarting if the slightest thing feels off. While this is happening, strangers are hounding her for using the 'wrong' bathroom. That makes the need to scrub herself off even stronger.

I wrap my fingers around the pinky finger of my partner Jess, a non-binary butch who very well might have OCD too. They've recommended I watch it, because it means more to them than any TV show ever has.

I squint my eyes and start to cry. What does it mean to have our stories softly told to us? To have a semi-fictional character tell you they *get it*, in a world that famously doesn't?

*Monday 4:55pm*
*i don't know what to do—the hand soap looks really strange in this restaurant bathroom. the label indicates the scent is chamomile, but the liquid inside is bright orange. that can't possibly be chamomile. maybe someone has replaced it with hydrochloric acid and orange food colouring? would i rather not use soap at all, or use the acid soap?*

*Monday 5:02pm*
*i'm remembering a news story i read about a man who was charged with putting acid in the hand soap dispensers at a gay bar. luckily he was caught before anyone got hurt. but i'm still feeling good about my decision not to properly wash my hands just before*

*but, great. now i'm panicked about being poisoned because nothing is safe and because i'm gay*

*Tuesday 11:37am*
*it was scary as fuck, but i just used the hand soap at work. the*
*colour was off and there was this weird condensation on the*
*inside of the bottle. it looked really terrifying. but i still used*
*it because i'm a tough bitch, i guess? nothing bad happened.*
*maybe not all mystery hand soap is acid. that is good news*

## When healing is horrifying, hopeful and hilarious

Perhaps the reason I try so hard to make my therapist laugh is to pay homage to the adage 'If you don't, you cry'.

That became exceptionally true when I moved into a house with two of my best friends, Tyler and Ash. They both understand my OCD to an extensive degree, having been close to me during the pointiest ends of my illness.

They know most of my triggers, and they help soothe my anxiety on the daily. Tyler and Ash know that lighters are particularly terrifying to me and that I avoid touching them at all costs. When we sit in the shed and drink a hundred wines and spend the evening yelling about Lady Gaga, they often argue about who gets to light my cigarette first. They push each other's arms down and scramble on their couch toward me, presenting their lighters like a first date holding out a rose. They know what glasses and ice trays are most comfortable, so take turns making me delicious cocktails that taste like safety.

When Jess, Tyler, Ash and I are in the same room, I feel seen. My symptoms are so understood they almost remain unspoken. An uneasy glance is enough for any of them to spring into action and soothe me. We wax lyrical about our therapists. We laugh about Safety Boy eating pepper.

We turn terrifying moments into hilarious ones. I'm never alien; my OCD is just part of the package deal of being my pal.

When Tyler was coming to terms with an OCD diagnosis

herself, we would yell across from our respective bedrooms the fucked-up intrusive thoughts we were having. We would scream from laughter about the most unhinged things our brains would cook up.

We would wonder out loud why we both watch *Law and Order: SVU* so much if we hate cops and know that viewing distressing content can cause both of our intrusive thoughts to kick it up into overdrive. We talk about how hot Mariska Hargitay looks in a singlet. We joke about things our therapists say, and create the most grotesque exposure therapy scenarios imaginable, just for kicks.

We laugh so hard together about our OCD that we cry. It creates a soothing dissonance from the sheer discomfort our illnesses bring.

Despite having some horrible housemates in the past, there have been many who have helped create a safe home to exist in.

At the start of Melbourne's first lockdown, I had four new housemates move in. I nervously sat them down in the first week and spoke to them. I'd planned the meeting days before. I told them that having OCD meant that I'd probably have separate crockery and pantry items. They may hear me check the doors numerous times, and I can't really share food or drinks.

I steeled myself for invasive questions and dismissal, but all I got was empathy and nonchalance.

'That's literally so fine, Dani,' one housemate said. 'I honestly thought you were going to try and recruit us into a multi-level marketing scheme.'

Falling in love with Jess while experiencing the height of my OCD symptoms has seen hour upon hour of being in bed crying. An unexpected experience with an unsafe drink or a screaming intrusive thought throws me into hysteria, while they give me scritchies and catch the tears off my face. We giggle when our brains go somewhere silly, and we help each other sit through the discomfort of exposure.

When it feels like the world doesn't understand you and your illness, even the smallest hint of acceptance can change everything. Between Jess, my best friends, my family and my genius therapist, I have more hints than I could need.

>*Saturday 11:40pm*
>
>*the uber driver offers me hand sanitiser and it's from a brand i don't recognise. he's holding it expectantly, but all i see is danger. it's a global pandemic, so it's rather uncouth to not take the offer. i freeze—all the worst-case scenarios are running through my head*
>
>*i eventually cave and take it, but immediately rub it all into my jeans. my jeans are now wet, and i can feel the moisture creeping into my thigh skin. i panic, completely expecting my hand and leg to set on fire, or for me to slowly pass out*
>
>*my therapist talks to me about sitting with the discomfort when i've been exposed to something horrifying. 'it's physiologically impossible for that discomfort and anxiety to stay that high forever,' he tells me. 'be patient, kind and soothing to yourself. you'll surprise yourself with how strong you really are.'*
>
>*my brain hates to accept that, hours later, nothing bad has happened. i am not in danger. there was never any threat*
>
>*Monday 12:17pm*
>*had random tomato sauce out of jess's fridge. didn't know where it was from, but i managed to eat it anyway and was really proud of myself. nothing bad happened*

Whenever I write about my anxiety, I reflect on how deeply it hinders me. I also reflect on how, in a twisted type of way, it can make me who I am. My most anxious thoughts can fuel my most creative moments. I'm wildly good in a crisis, because I'm constantly on high alert. My anxiety forces me to make choices for myself and prioritise my needs. When I expect the worst constantly, a positive outcome will always be a fun surprise.

I wouldn't wish it on my worst enemy, but I've developed ways to live with anxiety and accept it as a part of myself.

I've been trying to apply the same frameworks of thinking to OCD, and I hit a wall every time. Are there any ways that living with OCD make me a more creative or conscious person? No. Will I try to boil my complex and lengthy experiences into a single lesson that's taught me 'resilience'? Not at all.

Living with OCD is exceptionally difficult. My experiences are inextricably linked to fear and trauma. My symptoms permeate my everyday, with varying degrees of intensity.

But my illness isn't my whole self.

My OCD can feel like an annoying sidekick, who can be brought down by perseverance and audacity. When I'm at my strongest, I can notice and lovingly dismiss my intrusive thoughts. I let my obsessions run rampant while I resist a compulsion. I remind myself that my symptoms are explainable. My thoughts can't hurt me, and my strength to tackle them is only growing.

My experience isn't a medical mystery and there are countless others like me. They're on my TV having a meltdown in a public bathroom. They're across the hallway from me, and they're lying next to me in bed. They're on the same unhinged Google journey, finding scarf woman, Fictional Sandra and the man salaciously licking the bottom of a shoe. They're in the pages of this book. They're living an experience that feels so loud, but so unheard. They have stories like mine. They're facing their terrifying fears on the daily, even if the people around them don't see it.

Some days, my biggest challenge is a lumpy avocado. Others, it's leaving the house and stepping into a world that feels like it's made of cyanide.

I may not be a heterosexual woman wearing an oversized scarf, but I still experience joy. I can love and feel loved, and marvel in the pleasure of a purely unremarkable day.

Knowledge can really feel powerful. I understand my illness and I appreciate how difficult it is to manage. That means I can be kind to myself when I take three times as long to get myself a glass of water. I forgive myself when I succumb to the compulsions, and I celebrate myself every time I work through them.

Being open about my OCD has shifted the power back toward me. Taking therapy seriously has given me the strength I need to work through this. Connecting with people who understand me has given me a soft landing when I inevitably stumble.

And for everything else? There's always coconut hand cream and 'Murder on the Dancefloor'.

# Acknowledgements and Contributor Notes

While all views and perspectives contained in these pieces remain the authors' own, the authors and their editor, Georgia Richter, would like to acknowledge the input, guidance and expertise of OCD therapist Kimberley Quinlan in reviewing the stories in this collection and in providing her support, enthusiasm and her clinical perspective. It is much appreciated.

**Martin Ingle** is a writer, filmmaker, actor and obsessive-compulsive worrywart who lives and works on Yuggera land. His work spans all things documentary, fiction, theatre and mental health. His comedy-drama series *Disorderly* was developed through Screen Queensland in 2018 and among other gongs was an international finalist for the prestigious ScreenCraft Fellowship. Suffering from obsessive compulsive disorder to varying degrees of severity for many years, he is a fierce mental health advocate, featuring in the OCD episode of the ABC's *You Can't Ask That* in 2021, and playing the lead role (opposite a plush toy dinosaur) in the Screen Australia–developed series about OCD, *Plushed*. He's a contributor to mental health anthology *Admissions*, published by Upswell Publishing in 2022, and his other writing has been published in *The Guardian, ABC News Online, The Chaser* and *The Shovel*.

martindefinite.com
Facebook: @martindefinite
Instagram: @martindefinite

**Dani Leever** is a genderqueer nonfiction writer from Naarm. They're currently the Online Deputy Editor at Archer Magazine. They've been published in *Junkee*, Pedestrian.TV, SBS, *Voiceworks, Scum Mag, Broadsheet* and more. They previously sat on the *Voiceworks* Editorial Committee, and recently finished up as a staff writer for MTV. They write about gender, mental illness, pop culture and queerness. Outside writing, Dani performs as a genderbending drag DJ called DJ Gay Dad—they're extremely passionate about finding a song to match the BPM of 'Untouched' by The Veronicas.

Twitter: @DaniLeever

**Patrick Marlborough** is a neurodivergent nonbinary writer, comedian, journalist, critic and musician based in Walyalup (Fremantle), Whadjuk Boodja. They have been published in *VICE, Rolling Stone, The Guardian, The Saturday Paper, Junkee, Noisey, Meanjin, Overland, Crikey, The Lifted Brow, Cordite, Going Down Swinging, The Betoota Advocate*, and beloved other. They are a passionate mental health and disability advocate, regularly writing about their experiences with depression, suicide, bipolar, high functioning autism, and OCD. They have lived their whole life in Fremantle and spend their days arguing with their incredibly naughty dog, Buckley.

patrickmarlborough.com
Instagram: @cormac_mccafe
Twitter: @cormac_mccafe

**Katharine Pollock** is a Sydney-based writer who lives and writes on Eora land. Her debut novel, *Her Fidelity* (Penguin Random House, 2022), is the comedic story of a young(ish) woman working in a struggling Brisbane record shop and finding her place in the world. In 2021, Katharine completed her PhD exploring women in music and the confessional mode. She writes comedic personal essays and short stories. She was most recently published as part of the 2021 Microflix Writing Award and was the winner of GenreCon's 2021 short story competition. Katharine believes in the connective power of personal stories. She is represented by Zeitgeist Media.

Instagram: @thatrecordstoregirl

**Kimberley Quinlan** is a licensed marriage and family therapist who has a private practice in Calabasas, California, specialising in anxiety, OCD and related disorders, and eating disorders. Kimberley is the founder of CBTschool.com, an online psycho-education platform that provides online courses for those with obsessive compulsive disorder and body-focused repetitive behaviours. Kimberley is the author of *The Self-Compassion Workbook for OCD: Lean into Your Fear, Manage Difficult Emotions, and Focus on Recovery*, as well as the host of *Your Anxiety Toolkit* podcast, a podcast aimed at providing mindfulness-based tools for anxiety, OCD, depression and body-focused repetitive behaviours. Kimberley is known for her vibrant and mindful approach to mental health issues. She has been featured in many world-renowned and prestigious media outlets, such as *The Australian*, *The Washington Post*, *The LA Times*, *The Wall Street Journal*, NPR (National Public Radio), KCRW public radio and *The Seattle Times*.

kimberleyquinlan-lmft.com
Instagram: @youranxietytoolkit

**Sienna Rose Scully** is the youngest of four children. She is an Integrated Marketing Communications graduate who grew up in Noongar Whadjuk Boodja (Fremantle), Western Australia. Sienna obtained her bachelor's degree as a student-athlete where she played soccer at a collegiate level in the USA. She recently returned from living in Buenos Aires, Argentina with her fiancé, to move back to Fremantle. Along with diagnoses of depression and chronic anxiety, Sienna has dealt with OCD since childhood and is passionate about bringing awareness to what this disorder entails and to help other OCD sufferers.

Instagram: @siennascully
Email: siennascully1997@gmail.com